D1155305

Kierkegaard, Heidegger, Buber and Barth

JAMES BROWN

ORIGINALLY PUBLISHED AS
Subject and Object in Modern Theology

COLLIER BOOKS, NEW YORK, NEW YORK

FIRST COLLIER BOOKS EDITION 1962
THIRD PRINTING 1971

*The Croall Lectures
given in the University of Edinburgh
1953*

Kierkegaard, Heidegger, Buber and Barth was published in hardcover edition by The Macmillan Company under the title *Subject and Object in Modern Theology*

*The Macmillan Company, 866 Third Avenue,
New York, N.Y. 10022*

Printed in the United States of America

General Introduction

ONLY A SHORT generation ago it was still customary for theological thinking to be carried out within the framework of avowedly philosophical concepts, and philosophical theology was a fairly well-defined *genre* within the whole field of theology. The great work of nineteenth-century theology was carried out for the most part by scholars who had undergone intensive training in the idealist movement in philosophy. It is no derogation of the achievement of that time to say that this simple conjunction of two disciplines is no longer possible today. Many things have contributed so to change the picture of the work which theologians and philosophers have to do that it seems to be not so much a modified picture as an entirely new one. The strong blasts of positive and empirical dogmatic theology blowing down from Switzerland upon Europe and America, the immense changes which have overtaken philosophy, especially in Britain, so that the very ways of thinking seem to have altered, and the changes which have taken place in the world in which we all live—have all contributed to bring about this revolution. We live in a post-liberal, post-idealist, atomic age in theology. Philosophy and theology alike are being compelled to face their traditional problems in such a radical way that the question even arises: are our traditional problems the real ones?

In this situation it seems possible, however risky, to attempt a new facing of the problems of living in the mid-century world, not in the strength of isolated disciplines, but in a meeting of those disciplines on the common ground offered by our life in this world. The present Library of Philosophy and Theology, therefore, desires to offer a meeting-place for the thought of contemporary theologians and philosophers, Continental and Anglo-Saxon, yet without partisan or *a priori* assumptions about the way in which such a meeting may best be used.

Among the early volumes in the Library will come a study of existentialist theology as revealed in the work of Rudolf Bultmann: a collection of papers in philosophical theology as seen from the standpoint of the philosophers of logical analysis; an unfinished, posthumous work on ethics by Dietrich Bonhoeffer; and a volume of essays on philosophical, literary and theological themes by Rudolf Bultmann.

No doctrinaire scheme underlies this first choice of titles, nor the editorial plans. If the matter may be summed up provocatively and negatively, the editorial assumption of the series is that neither the idealist nor the linguistic philosophy, neither the liberal nor the neo-Calvinist nor the neo-Thomist theology, is able by itself to speak properly to the needs of our time, or to the demands which we are aware of as flowing out of our historical situation from the Renaissance onwards. We may hope that the volumes to be produced in this series, whether coming from the philosophical or the theological camp, will in fact not speak of or to any mere "camp." They will have as their concern the possibilities offered to the world through the tradition both of philosophical thinking and of Christian history.

R. GREGOR SMITH

Contents

Author's Note

AUTHOR'S NOTE

The author desires to express his deep sense of the honour done him by the Trustees in appointing him to the Croall Lectureship for 1952-53, and his gratitude for the kindness shown him by the Principal and the Staff of New College, Edinburgh during the delivery of the Lectures there.

COLMONELL MANSE   JAMES BROWN
AYRSHIRE
JULY 1955

To the Memory of my Mother
JANET REID
1868–1954

"This question has two sides," he said. "An Objective side, and a Subjective side. Which are we to take"?

He had had a German education as well as a French . . . the original English foundation showing through every now and then . . .

"Take the Objective view first . . . What do we know? . . . Do you mean to deny the Objective view, so far? Very well, then . . . Now arguing in this way, from within outwards, what do we reach? We reach the Subjective view. I defy you to controvert the Subjective view. Very well, then . . . what follows? The Objective-Subjective explanation follows, of course"!

Wilkie Collins, The Moonstone, 1868

Chapter 1

The Subject-Object Relation

Introduction and Terminology

IN THE FOREGROUND of Holbein's painting known as *The Ambassadors* in the National Gallery in London there stretches across the tiled floor between the feet of the two human figures a curious amorphous object which at first sight baffles identification. If one can contrive to stand close to the right-hand side of the picture and look diagonally down its length the mysterious object foreshortens into the likeness of a human skull. Now in the native language of the artist a skull can be called "a hollow bone"—*ein hohl Bein*. We have here, therefore, a piece of pictorial punning upon the artist's surname, Holbein's signature in a rebus. This is an example of what in Shakespeare's time was called a "perspective," several allusions to which occur in his plays. Thus in *King Richard Second* (II. ii. 18) we read of

> "perspectives, which when rightly gaz'd upon
> Show nothing but confusion; ey'd awry
> Distinguish form."

"Merely fanciful effects in painting were welcome to Elizabethan taste," writes Lionel Cust.[1] "Among these ranked high certain paintings in perspective, *a tour de force* in which some painters were wont to practise their skill . . . these distorted figures . . . can only be seen aright by looking through a hole in a slanting direction."

This course of lectures proposes to look at certain trends in modern theology from the perspective viewpoint of the Subject-Object relation and the antithesis therefrom derived of subjective versus objective thinking. It is not anticipated that so viewed all or even many of the confusions in the theological scene will forthwith collapse into intelligibility.

[1] *Shakespeare's England*, Vol. II, p. 10.

The distortions in an Elizabethan "perspective" were, as stated, *a tour de force* of intentional misrepresentation, calculated by a highly skilled artist to make sense from a standpoint known and allowed for in advance. The variations in latter-day theology are not a calculated confusion: they are the inevitable result of varying presuppositions and approach in different and differing theologians. There is no guarantee, therefore, that the attempt to view these variations from the perspective pin-hole of the Subject-Object relation must yield edifying results. But there are certain features in the theological scene which suggest that this approach might bring about some useful clarifications. Four such matters may be here mentioned.

In the first place: the Subject-Object relation, whatever its metaphysical or ontological status, is at least one of the fundamentals of epistemology. Not to anticipate later discussion, I venture to think it would generally be allowed that truth will involve some sort of correct relation or proportion between these two elements in knowing, Subject and Object—not necessarily an identical relation or proportion in all kinds of knowing—and that human thinking is liable to distortion when this correct balance is upset on the one side or the other, in the peculiar circumstances of the kind of reality investigated. Theology is certainly a human inquiry, whether or not it be more, whatever its assurance of a more than human reference and validity in the objects with which it deals or the methods by which it deals with them. It is to be expected, therefore, that theology, too, will share in that error which is common to humanity, and that sometimes such error will be the result of a disproportion of the subjective and objective factors in its special kind of knowledge.

In the second place: the modern world has arrived at a distinction between subjective and objective thinking, which in its popular version at least tends to identify truth with objectivity and error with subjectivity. Is this a valid development? Or is it an example of what we have mentioned as a general possibility: the overstressing of one side of the knowledge relation? Is it, by any chance, a confusion resulting from a failure to understand that, within the all-embracing Subject-Object relation which is fundamental to knowledge as such, there is room for variation, according to the matters studied, in the contribution which each side makes to the result? Elimination of the subjective may be a virtue in natural science; would it be a virtue in poetry, which one of its most eminent practitioners has described as "the breath and finer spirit of all knowledge"? This question is not to be lightly raised or answered; for obviously poetry, too, envisages some sort of "control by the object" as the test of its truth. Indeed, a modern movement in music and painting in Germany had for its slogan *die neue Sachlichkeit*, the "new objectivity" (almost "thingitude" or "thingness"). What is the affiliation of theology here, with science or with art? The question is complicated in the case of Christian theology in particular, where a special relationship of its truth to *history* is asserted. And unfortunately, just as we might have asked the historians what is the nature of the kind of truth in which they deal, it would appear that they are not very sure that they can tell us.

In the third place: this general possibility has been particularized for modern theology by the momentous affirmation of Soren Kierkegaard that "the passion of the infinite is precisely subjectivity, and thus subjectivity becomes the truth." Made over one hundred years ago this thesis of the *Concluding Unscientific Postscript*,[2] 1846, has produced results of the most varied sort. The influence of Kierkegaard is clearly traceable throughout the whole movement of thought labelled Existentialism, one of whose recurring notes is an emphasis on *decision*, i.e. on a volitive factor in the process of arriving at truth. Existentialism is properly a movement in philosophy, and its religious bearing is not immediately apparent. It has a theistic conclusion in Kierkegaard himself (although it is doubtful whether in his case the conclusion to religious faith is based on his form of Existentialism) as also in Gabriel Marcel, but a non-theistic conclusion in Heidegger and an atheistic in Sartre. There is a new awareness in all quarters of the relevance of the thinker to his thought, and in that sense, of the Subject to the Object of his thought. Theologians have been asking whether this philosophical discussion throws any light on the *faith* which they have all

[2] E. T., Swenson and Lowrie, 1941, p. 181.

along known to be the organ of spiritual knowledge. In what sense is the exhortation "Have faith in God" an invitation to the exercise of man's subjectivity? And what is the relevance in this connection of warnings against "wishful thinking" from the side of psychology?

Lastly, in the fourth place: a profound influence has been exercised upon Christian theology recently by a type of thinking which stresses subjectivity in another fashion, one which we may call, from the title of its most notable manifesto, the "I and Thou" philosophy deriving from Martin Buber. Here the insistence that thought must take on an entirely different complexion, according as it confronts mere *objects* or other *subjects* of thought and experience, has come as a very revelation to many in our time, clearing away obstacles to belief in the validity of morality and religion which had formerly looked like necessities of thought. Partly in line with this way of thinking the theology of Karl Barth frequently declares that "God is always Subject," and "the Subject which is never Object" is a recurrent formula in the theology of an allied school.

For these reasons, therefore, it looks as if it might be a not unprofitable venture to attempt a sketch of the development of the Subject-Object relation, together with that of the associated terminology of subjectivity and objectivity, subjective and objective thinking, through certain outstanding thinkers of the last hundred years who have particularly influenced Christian theology. The recurrence of this language in writers so various as Buber and Barth, Heidegger and Tillich, to name only a few, certainly suggests that theology is here preoccupied with an identical problem of fundamental gravity. It is hoped that the results will be more than a clarification of terminology—although even that would still be worth while. Whether the larger problem of insight into the nature of the truth of the Christian religion is in any way served must await the performance itself.

Before we go further it may be well to consider a possible objection which might be taken to our undertaking *in limine*. Are you not virtually proposing, someone might ask, to set up a philosophical criterion of theological truth? Have you not in mind some sacrosanct standard of the contributions permissible from the sides of Subject and Object respectively to an ideal of truth, a standard which will condemn *this* development as seeking an inappropriate objectivity, this other as an exercise of irrational subjectivity, in the religious context? Are you not proposing to throw away one of the most precious gains in the revival of Protestant theology in our time, the principle that the gospel is not accountable to any standards of truth but its own?

Whether such a fear is or is not justified must, of course, wait on the detail of the argument to follow. Meanwhile I would agree that there is a sense in which theology must be allowed to have its own standards of truth, and that these will not be the standards of a philosophy which would rule out the possibility of *any* theology in advance. It does not seem to me that a discussion of a philosophical terminology widely in use in modern theology necessarily involves importation of unsympathetic criteria into theology. But it is perhaps well to be forewarned of a danger.

On the other hand it is not immediately obvious to what the principle that "theology must be allowed to have its own standards of truth" commits us or what it permits to us. We may well be suspicious of talk about "rationality in general." We have come to a vivid awareness of how intimately in any inquiry method is dictated by the matter studied. But I find I cannot free myself from the conviction that reason is in some sort the same structure of mind no matter in what material it is exercised. It is not a question, in the special matter that interests us here, of philosophy versus theology. It is a matter rather of the mind operating philosophically within theology. Certain concerns of mind are philosophical whether these arise within science or theology: the definition, the distinction, is given by the method, the attitude, the level, at which the discussion is conducted. Theology may be more or less philosophical: it is entirely doubtful whether it can cease to be philosophical without ceasing to be what has hitherto been known as theology.

Considerable prominence is being given at the moment to a controversy on the Continent about "demythologizing the Bible." This is the up-to-date version of an old story. Rudolf Bultmann draws attention to the presence of a deal of antiquated science in the framework within which saving truth is presented—the "three-decker universe" of heaven, earth and hell, the demoniacal possession theory of disease, and allied views of the mechanics of inspiration and the processes of salvation. Certainly there is a problem here for the modern presentation of Bible truth. But it might equally well be emphasized that the Bible contains much of the philosophy of the ancient world, and that this presents a similar problem and task. Whoever uses words philosophizes, will he nill he; for language is the vehicle of conscious reason. "Let us not forget," says Karl Barth, "that theology in fact, so surely as it avails itself of human speech, is also a philosophy or a conglomerate of all sorts of philosophy."[3] A metaphysic of being, a view of the scheme of things in space and time enters into the elements and structure of language—a truth which finds distorted recognition in a current attempt to turn philosophy into a branch of semantics, as well as in the fashionable philosophical method of "analysis." The Bible cannot dissociate itself from this fate. We may hold the implicit philosophy of language to be "the metaphysics of common sense." Unless this is itself to be taken as the ultimate to which sophistication must eventually return after devious wanderings, the question must be raised how far biblical truth is compromised thereby. And, of course, there are the more explicit borrowings and influences from Greek, Persian and other sources. Is the philosophizing implicit in biblical theology to be conceived as in a class by itself, and so exempt from philosophic self-criticism? One thing seems certain: biblical theology itself can not be erected into the final criterion. Some of the most impressive and valuable work in modern biblical studies lies precisely in this field. One thinks of the monumental *Theologisches Wörterbuch* in process of publication under the editorship of G. Kittel. One thinks of the fructifying influence of such a work as O. Cullmann's *Christ and Time* upon theology generally. The particularity of the Bible's own views of time and history, sin, grace, justification and sanctification, on human psychology and personality (especially in its relation to the body); all these topics and many more are in process of

[3] *Church Dogmatics*, E. T., I, 1. 188.

receiving definition from a superb degree of scholarship never before equalled. When the task is completed—assuming it to be capable of completion—what then? Is biblical theology to take over from all the other theological disciplines as the norm of Christian truth in all spheres of thought and practice? Is this what is meant by those who desiderate for the body of Christian truth to which they would profess allegiance that it should be simply "biblical" instead of bearing the label of any particular theological school or party? Would this not be a fundamentalism of a new, if more refined kind? An inerrant, supernaturally guaranteed biblical theology would involve the infallibility of these ancient authors on matters where theology and philosophy overlap or mutually involve each other. Is this what is meant by conserving the permanent elements in the biblical view of God, man and the world? I am glad to be able to align myself with Karl Barth once again on this question. "The inquiry concerning Biblical doctrine as the basis of our language about God falls upon *exegetical* theology. It must also be kept continually before the eyes of dogmatics. But the proper basis of Christian language is identical with its proper content, only in God and not for us. Therefore dogmatics as such does not inquire what the Apostles and Prophets have said, but what we ourselves must say 'on the basis of the Apostles and Prophets.' This task cannot be taken from us, even by the knowledge of the 'scripture basis' which necessarily precedes it . . . the Church recognizes the claim upon her . . . to ask, in view of this basis of all Christian language, with the utter seriousness of one who does not yet know, *what* Christian language ought to say and should say today."[4]

If we agree, then, that the assets of Christian theology cannot be "frozen" at the biblical level of terminology and the thought-forms therein implied, it is difficult to see how the self-reflection of thought upon its own nature can be disallowed in theology, merely because this process can be called philosophical. Exactly how relevant, how much or how little worth while an examination of the Subject-Object relation as it figures in modern theology may turn out to be, cannot be determined in advance of the experiment. Our

[4] *op. cit.* 16f.

scruples may prove to have been needless anxiety. It may be that this relation, instead of being the fixed quantum it has the air of being, may prove surprisingly variable in different contexts. So far from being any sort of invulnerable, self-sufficient criterion of truth apart from the material in which it is realized, it may be seen to be a comparative abstraction, with its own differentiations within science *and* theology; in which event the fear of foreign interference will have lost its sting.

That to us it seems incredible that men should ever *not* have known that knowledge implies and involves the Subject-Object relation, or that they should ever have failed to express the relation in this terminology, is testimony to the influence of the Critical Philosophy of Immanuel Kant. If the immanent philosophy of language has always implied this distinction and relation of Subject and Object; if the systems of ancient Greece and western Europe have all along worked with some consciousness of this fundamental structure of human thought; if it appears as the substance of the problem which engaged reflection from Descartes' distinction of thinking and material substance down to Hume; still it was only in Kant that the modern formulation of the relation clearly emerged and that the terminology in which we still discuss the problems of the relationship was fixed. As regards this last, it comes to us as a surprise to find that the modern use of the terms "subjective" and "objective," deriving from Kant, precisely reverses their original use in the medieval schoolmen. The history of these terms is interestingly set forth by Rudolf Eucken in his *Main Currents of Modern Thought*. "Duns Scotus (d. 1308)," he writes,[5] "first employed them as technical terms and in opposing senses. 'The word subjective was applied to whatever concerned the subject-matter of the judgement, that is, the concrete objects of thought; on the other hand the term objective referred to that which is contained in the mere *obicere* (i.e. in the presenting of ideas) and hence qualifies the presenting subject' (see Prantl, *Geschichte der Logik im Abendlande*, iii, 208). Philosophy employed the expressions in these senses until the seventeenth and eighteenth centuries; but the counter-

[5] *op. cit.*, 35, E. T., 1912.

term to objective (which was more commonly used than subjective) was more often *formaliter* or *realiter*. The systems which carried on the scholastic philosophy show, at this period, a change in the use of *objectivus* which paved the way for the more modern terminology. The complete reversal of meaning did not take place, however, until the words were assimilated into the German language (through the Wolffian school of philosophy). At first the terms *subjektivisch* and *objektivisch* . . . were not used outside this school . . . It was the Kantian philosophy which first brought them into common use, and at the beginning of the nineteenth century they were widely employed. It was entirely owing to German influence that their new meanings became general, and at first they were frequently regarded as strange." A glance at the *Oxford English Dictionary* corroborates this German origin of the English usage. It was Coleridge, that great popularizer of the Kantian transcendental philosophy in England, who first introduced his fellow-countrymen to the terms "subjective" and "objective" in their new meanings, and who proceeded to make rewarding use of them in the realm of literary criticism. A quotation from the *Biographia Literaria*, indeed, will form no bad introduction to our terminological discussion.[6] "All knowledge rests upon the coincidence of an object with a subject . . . The sum of all that is merely objective we will call nature . . . the sum of all that is subjective we may comprehend in the name of the self, of intelligence . . . During the act of knowledge itself the objective and the subjective are so instantly united that we cannot determine to which of the two priority belongs . . . Self-consciousness is not a kind of being, but a kind of knowing."

There are several points in this, Coleridge's own explanation of his use of "subjective" and "objective," which deserve notice. First, it is aware that in Kant the distinction between Subject and Object and their conjunction in the knowledge relation is a matter of epistemology—of analysis of the nature and conditions of knowledge—not, in the first instance, of metaphysics or ontology—description of the

[6] I owe this quotation to Mary Colum, wife of the Irish poet, in her *From these Roots*, 1941, p. 73f.

nature of being or reality. Secondly, it is only in appearance that we cut the feet from under this distinction by observing against Coleridge that "self-consciousness" or simply "consciousness"[7] *is* a "kind of being," namely, psychical being, and that knowledge implies knowing minds. Coleridge is right that knowledge is a different kind of being from psychological occurrence in an empirical self. Thirdly, Coleridge's identification of "the sum of all that is subjective" with "the self," and "the sum of all that is . . . objective" with "nature," is itself a development beyond strict epistemology; it adds concrete determinations to the Kantian Subject and Object of an ontological character, the nature of which we shall shortly try to describe.

Meanwhile we return to the primary fact about Kant's statements on Subject and Object, namely that they are epistemological theory. He is concerned to determine the nature and "transcendental" conditions of knowledge in general, and to lay down the conditions *a priori* of the necessity which attaches to the kind of knowledge which belongs to mathematical and physical science. To the generalities of all knowledge, then, belongs this fact, that it involves the appearance of an Object to a Subject, in a unique kind of relation which is constituted by their togetherness, in which each implies the other. In this context the Subject is not yet an existent; it is a logical (or epistemological) presupposition. The question of its nature and existence is "bracketed," to use the terminology of the Phenomenology of E. Husserl, for a similar process in determining the pure forms of thought. It seems to myself that two things need to be said about the Kantian epistemology at this stage. Firstly, the question of *existence* of the Subject *is* postponed. Kant is quite aware of this problem, and it is common to sum up his position here in the doctrine of the three egos—the logical, the empirical, and the transcendental. I do not know that it is possible to make statements about any one of these without involving the others. Kant does stand for the common-sense position that thought implies a thinker. Moreover, the famous "synthetic unity of apperception" which constitutes "objects" for the understanding, involves an activity which must be

[7] So Mary Colum, *ad. loc.*

located in an agent of some sort—presumably a psychical agent. Epistemology implies existence, and the latter involves a metaphysics of some sort. Kant's own metaphysics are not unfairly described as dualistic, in line with the Cartesian dualism of thinking and material substance. But this is not an inevitable consequence of the distinction of Subject and Object. It is a going on to conceive that "existence" must needs be of the same order on both sides of the distinction, that the Subject must be a "substance," even if a different kind of substance from the Object. Moreover, the actually existing epistemological Subject is still not "the empirical ego." This last is a concrete existent in the sphere of psychical fact, a particular mind with distinguishing qualities of acumen or obtuseness, receiving qualifications which we can only describe as moral, e.g. attentiveness, application, patience, reliability; all of which are distinguishable from the synthesizing activity of mind as such. None of these things are part of the strictly conceived Kantian Subject. But secondly, Kant's Object is equally involved existentially in his Subject. He certainly believes in the existence of "things-in-themselves." But the Objects of knowledge are interpenetrated by thought, and we cannot think away thought from being by an effort of thought. The synthetic unity of apperception involves being in a perspective for mind. There have been those in recent times who have thought that nothing is easier than to think away thought by the simple denial that consciousness "exists": "mind" is a cross-section or perspective of objects. Both "cross-section" and "perspective" surely imply a centre or standpoint from which a view is taken, and therefore a mutual implication and interpenetration of thought and being. The synthetic unity of apperception is a togetherness in relation which is realized in every single concept, every knitting together of the components of an "object," every act of judgement, every intellectual generalization which introduces order into phenomena. But does all this not belong as much to the side of the Object as to that of the Subject of knowledge? In Kantian terms "objectivity" belongs to Objects in relation to Subjects: it is not the objectivity of "things-in-themselves." Even if we escape from his dualistic metaphysics can we ever hope to transcend the mutual implication of thought and being? This question abides for others than Kantians, and is a perpetual warning against easy claims to have reached "objectivity."

Neither Subject nor Object being simple self-contained entities existing in their own sufficiency, according to the Kantian scheme, it follows that existence cannot be sub-divided straight away into "subjective" and "objective" spheres of being. Subject and Object are poles of a relation, and either, taken by itself, is an abstraction. The Subject, in particular, is a point—the needle's eye through which the threads of relation pass, according to the favourite metaphor of idealism. The epistemological point, like the geometrical, has position but no magnitude. For the Subject to possess any concrete qualities it must have some surface to which these can adhere. To say that it is a synthesizing activity is to attribute to it a nature of sorts, as we have seen; this is to bring the Subject within sight of the world of psychical reality. To call the Subject "self or intelligence" with Cole-ridge is to go still further in this direction. (Incidentally, it is to bring the Subject within the possible Objects of its own knowledge!) To call the world of the "objective" by the name of "nature" is to complete the distinction of existents into the two great classes of mental and non-mental, minds and "things" which appear to minds. Subjective and objective have become two departments of reality, of which different qualities and characteristics can be predicated. Things and activities can now be described as more or less subjective or objective, according as they partake more or less of the nature of the knowing Subject or intelligence or mind on the one hand, or more or less of the matter presented to mind, of things or nature or "objects" in the narrower sense, re-spectively. And it cannot be too strongly asserted that *how* this distinction will be carried out in practice will depend, not on the simple Subject-Object relation which is a presup-position of epistemological analysis, but on considerations ultimately of a metaphysical kind about which argument and difference of opinion is at least possible. Thus we are launched upon the tossing sea of multitudinous distinction in the modern use of the antithesis of "subjective" and "objective" as a qualitative description of ways of thinking, acting and feeling, with valuations of approbation or opprobrium thereto attached.

"The exact significance of these terms in modern terminology, though distinct enough from that they bore in the Middle Ages," writes Eucken,[8] "is in itself most uncertain." The first meaning of subjective is that which pertains to the mere individual act of presentation; but it frequently means, especially when employed by scientists, anything and everything which a feeling and a thinking creature experiences in itself; also all convictions extending beyond the immediate evidence of the facts are called subjective and are regarded as a species of mere trimming. Thus what is deepest and what is shallowest are treated as of equal value. The term objective is also ambiguous. Sometimes it refers to objects as contrasted with mental activity, sometimes as constitutive of mind itself. Goethe aimed at objectivity; so does modern naturalism." Fortunately our task is not to draw up an exhaustive list of such variations and shades of meaning in the terms subjective and objective and to relate them to the parent distinction in the Kantian philosophy. Were that so, we might find ourselves in a similar situation to that which the late Professor John Laird mentions at the beginning of his Glasgow Gifford Lectures[9] with regard to variations in the meaning of the distinction between "natural" and "unnatural." "I have seen a list of such meanings that resembled the scoring sheet of a long innings at cricket, and I concluded that the batsman was still not out. His precise score was 61." It will suffice for our purpose to discuss a limited range of such meanings which have special relevance to our theological interest, and to indicate briefly the development involved.

In an endeavour to chart this sea of meaning we return to Kant, in the complexities and ambiguities of whose thought many of the later variations are already implicit. We have already noticed that for Kant the Subject soon ceases to be a bare point of epistemological presupposition. It is an activity of synthesis: we may even say that it has a certain structure, purely within the context of knowledge. When it gets to grips

[8] loc. cit.
[9] Theism and Cosmology, 1940, p. 41.

with the manifold of sensation in space and time this activity takes shape in the categories of the understanding. If the Subject has no superficies, no epidermis, it may be said to possess a skeleton, an articulate structure, in the list of the categories. Now Kant laid great stress upon the claim that his critical analysis of the nature of knowledge constituted a "Copernican revolution" in philosophy. Instead of viewing knowledge as a passive conformity of thought to objects complete in themselves apart from thought, which reflected themselves in the mirror of mind, objects were now required to submit themselves to the constitution and structure of mind in order to arrive at the organization of necessary knowledge. Here, if you care, is an assertion of the pre-eminence of the Subject, which is the fountain-head of the later assertion that "subjectivity is truth." Unfortunately this primacy of the Subject is viewed as a means to an end by definition or presupposition exalted above it, namely, necessary knowledge. "How is knowledge *a priori* possible"? is the question Kant sets out to answer; and Kant's reply is that mathematics and physics and the natural sciences derive their irrefragable necessity from the obligation of their contents to submit to the structure of the human mind for elaboration and interconnection. The human spirit, however —which is a different thing from the human mind—may have intimations of other orders of being and reality than those studied by the natural sciences; but what these last don't know isn't knowledge! Morality is the grand case in point with Kant. The categorical imperative of duty is obvious to the man on the moral level: it has the rational characteristics of necessity and universality, and so is reason in its practical aspect. But its implicates of freedom, immortality, God, go beyond anything we can *know* to what we can only *believe;* furthermore, freedom contradicts the necessity which reigns throughout the world of nature or phenomenal world, including the empirical self. Thus Kant can be held at one and the same time the source of the use of the term "objective" for what satisfies the canons of natural science and is "true" knowledge (with the possibility that the "subjective" is a *wrong* application of the conditions of knowledge, i.e. is error or illusion) and also of the view that there are present in the Subject in its larger reality grounds for going beyond nature, in moral and aesthetic experience particularly, to glimpses of a wider range of being and a more comprehensive truth than knowledge strictly so-called. Back and forward between these two poles his thought sways, his terminology determined by the more limited view of truth, but the total impression being that of something greater and grander, with flashes of the mystic disturbing the methodistical precisian of the Enlightenment.

To arrive at a state of affairs in which it is possible to say "subjectivity is truth" or "only objective thinking is true" is to have passed beyond Kant. For him all thinking, true or false, is both objective and subjective at once, because it is the meeting of a Subject and an Object in the unique relation in which truth and error are both possibilities, in which reality takes on the form of ideality. When we say that error occurs when the Subject loses touch with the Object, asserts itself apart from "control" by the Object, mistaking its own whims or illusions for "external" reality, we have in all these statements deserted the pure epistemological Subject and Object for various embodiments of concrete thinking; the Subject is now psychologically qualified, and we are speaking in terms of some particular view of the relations of the knowing self to its world—a view which, if it is wise, will allow for varying proportions of what is now called "subjectivity" and "objectivity" in the truth of which various subject-matters are capable. For example, the Object is no longer "external" in psychology when mind studies itself. Yet psychology aims at objectivity in its study or investigation of subjectivity. It attempts to be a natural science, proceeding by observation and experiment and verification, within the presupposition of the uniformity of nature. Whether and how far it succeeds is another matter. To an outsider, no study seems more uncertain of its fundamental concepts, what this self is that is studied, than the welter of disciplines that nowadays profess to deal with the psyche—psychology, analytic and behaviouristic, psycho-analysis in its rival schools of Freud, Adler and Jung, with its practical offshoots in psychotherapy. Kant himself wanted to assert both freedom and necessity of the Self, with no prejudice either to science or morals. If we are not content to hand over freedom to an unknowable *noumenon* we must draw the conclusion that to be an Object for a Subject does not mean that all Objects must be of the same kind, namely, the kind which submit themselves to sufficient and exhaustive description in terms of the categories of the understanding. Natural science deals with one class of Objects only; and regretfully we must surrender the ambition to speak of these others with the same kind of necessity in our generalizations which makes scientific statement so impressive. This is not to surrender the claim to "objectivity," however; nor is it to disparage the Subject-Object relation in favour of some other, e.g. to contrast knowledge with "intuition." Knowledge survives in intuition, and there is always a Subject and an Object present in any kind of awareness: only, awareness is not always of the "scientific" kind. In the nature of the case awareness must have these two poles, something knows something else. But the Kantian list of categories does not exhaust the operations of possible concatenation in the manifold of given reality, which goes beyond sensation. As regards "objectivity," all kinds of knowledge are of Objects, and truth is adequacy to the nature of the Object. "Control by the Object" is the touchstone of sanity versus illusion or delusion. But not all Objects are presented ready-made to the Subject's acceptance (none are, strictly speaking, according to Kant!). Some Objects are, include, involve, relations of the concrete Subject or self to its Objects; and to say that these Objects must either submit themselves to exhaustive description of the kind appropriate to natural science is not a legitimate deduction from an analysis of the Subject-Object relation of knowledge, but a piece of metaphysics of an unwarrantable kind, a conscious or unconscious presupposition arising from some other source, something *herangebracht*, intruded from the outside. It will definitely *not* do to identify "objectivity" with this control by Objects of a special sort, however difficult it may prove to establish tests of "objectivity"—tests of truth, in short—in such spheres as those of art, morality and religion.

What is the "objective" reality which the self articulates in moral or aesthetic judgements, in terms of which the truth of these may be determined? A major movement of thought in our time says that there is no such objective reality, that all such expressions are not so much judgements as ejaculations, utterances of feeling, with only a limited or induced generality, and properly to be punctuated with an exclamation mark at their close. The affirmations of religion are classed by Logical Positivism along with those of aesthetics and ethics as in the strict sense of the word "non-sense," beyond logical control or verification. Whether they are also to be dismissed as "nonsense" in the ordinary sense of the word does not appear to be finally decided.[10] Logical Positivism approximates to that side of Kant's philosophy for which the transcendent use of reason is illegitimate, and the *noumenal* realities or morals and religion are not possible objects of knowledge. It differs from Kant in that the latter regards moral and religious faith as still rational, the use of reason in its practical aspect, and its affirmations as of universal validity and therefore "objective" in the wider sense of pointers to ultimate reality, not the projections of caprice or wishful thinking. Short of morality and religion, what is the "truth" of art? Obviously this consists of a new balance of subjective and objective factors. The sphere of subjectivity is immensely increased and predominant in artistic creation and expression, in the sense that the personality of the individual artist counts for much towards the finished result. But artistic subjectivity has still its "objects." In surrealism these may be the subconscious depths of human personality. All art, moreover, is "objectification," the creation of its own world of "objects," even when these are the symbols of the most private and personal reactions of the artist's own subjectivity to his world of things and persons. And whether as "expression" or "communication" art aims furthermore at bodying forth some glimpse of the nature of things, of reality ultimate or proximate. Even in its most fantastic eccentricities it usually claims to be revelation, disclosure of truth, and in that sense "objective."

All use, therefore, of the label "objectivity" as the guarantee of truth depends upon a frame of reference, philosophical, scientific, artistic, moral, religious, which prescribes

[10] I understand that in L. Wittgenstein, one of the sources of this movement, they are not so dismissed.

what is relevant in its particular connection. The claim that certain "objects" alone are "real" and certain truths or kinds of truth only are "objective" without qualification, is a position that can only proceed from prejudice, when it is unreflective, or prejudgement when it is philosophical. In Kant's own system, from which the terms "subjective" and "objective" take their modern origin, the scales seem heavily weighted in favour of scientific naturalism: the mathematical and physical sciences in their application to nature are the type of knowledge, and their objects real beyond a doubt. But this is semblance only. Kant is sure of the moral law within his breast as equally self-authenticating in its majestic and even numinous splendour with the starry heavens above. If he seems to rest assurance of God, freedom and immortality on the inferior testimony of faith rather than knowledge, we may see in this the effects of a ready-made metaphysics which he brought to his task, which presupposed that knowledge is of phenomena only. What is this but to say that he held without argument to the existence of *noumenal* reality? With the Epistle to the Hebrews he held that "things which are seen were not made of things which do appear."[11] The entire scheme of things is not explicable in terms of natural science, nor is final truth bound by its conception of objectivity.

We conclude our terminological discussion with three reflections. Firstly: terminologically the current usage of Subject and Object is surprisingly modern, deriving from the technicalities of the Kantian critical philosophy. Some ambiguities in varying modern usage may derive from the fact that the terms are older, and that the modern precisely reverses the medieval usage. We require to bear in mind also that the terminology has an independent life of its own in grammar, where "subject" has a connotation of activity and "object" of passivity, with suggestions of the division of reality between animate and inanimate, between agents and things. And common-sense philosophy has a bias in favour of the superior reality of the material world of things that can be seen, handled, and even knocked about—witness Dr. Johnson's "refutation" of Berkeley! Philosophical usage de-

[11] Heb. II. 3.

riving from Kant is thus criss-crossed with memories of other, more ancient and more popular usages. For example, I trust I am not alone in occasionally boggling at such a phrase as "the subject of this discourse." "Subject" or "Object" of discourse? "Subject-matter" has to be called in to evade the ambiguity.

Secondly: a reminder of the epistemological status of the distinction between Subject and Object, that of itself the distinction solves no ontological problems, is provided by the figure it cuts in the version of absolute idealism presented by F. H. Bradley, a version which to him seemed self-evident but would now be rejected with scorn in many quarters. Mr. Bradley held that "to be real, or even barely to exist, must be to fall within sentience."[12] Reality, in short, is experience. But he also held that reality evades the distinction between Subject and Object at two levels, one below, the other above the plane of knowledge. At the lower end of the scale of degrees of reality we have the undifferentiated unity of felt experience, which, in the words of another expositor,[13] "we proceed, in the exercise of relational thought, to analyse into the known world of self and not-self, with all its manifold objects and distinctions. Combining the primitive experience of felt unity with the later experience of known diversity, we can recognize the latter as a transitional stage, and reach the idea of a higher experience, in which thought shall, as it were, return to the immediacy of feeling." Thus we reach the idea of the absolute experience, which conception of the nature of final reality is no exclusive property of European idealism deriving from Hegel, but is a commonplace of mysticism, eastern and western alike. We live in an age of conflicting realisms, for which nothing is so evident as that Bradley's self-evident presupposition must be rejected with vigour and his final conclusion with doubt. Instead of allowing everything to be swallowed up in mind or experience it is easier to doubt "Does consciousness exist"? and to give rein to an unbridled objectivity. Either way we are reminded that the conclusion disappoints the expectation of the

---

[12] *Appearance and Reality*, p. 144.
[13] A. S. Pringle-Pattison, *Man's Place in the Cosmos*, 1902, p. 104.

sixteenth to the eighteenth centuries that the nature of reality would disclose itself to a preliminary analysis of the nature of knowledge. The ultimate questions are still on our hands after we have distinguished between Subject and Object and arrived at the marvel of the "synthetic unity of apperception."

Thirdly, and lastly for the present: passing from the substantive to the adjectival form of the distinction, "subjectivity" and "objectivity" tell us very little of themselves. There is no absolute or standard norm of each, as it were, in an abstract ideal of truth in all kinds of matter. The Subject never is in any actual discipline a mere abstract point or featureless activity. In some studies its virtue as a concrete thinking agent may be to efface itself before the Object; in others its own contribution, or the contribution of the whole self of which the thinking self is only a part, to the Object is the whole point of the proceeding. All this without prejudice to the distinction between truth and error, sanity and delusion, capricious distortion and patient waiting upon the "facts." "Objectivity" in the sense of "truth" is the aim of all knowledge. In a discipline like theology, where so many and various factors are involved, which is so obviously a matter of outward and inward, of experience and history, perhaps of matters which transcend both, we must be prepared to encounter special difficulties in deciding what version of subjective and objective elements seems best to meet its case. At all events, our discussion should have delivered us from false standards of objectivity, from the fear of a criterion which can rule out religious faith in advance as "mere subjectivity." Any matter of rational inquiry must be allowed a certain elbow-room or breathing-space, as it were, in which to develop its own canons of intelligibility, to define its own kind of objectivity, to which it pretends in the name of truth. Whether or not this is compatible with other kinds of objectivity, scientific, philosophical, religious, and if not, whether and which must give way to which other as the more fundamental, all this is a question to which different minds will give different answers. Beneath all surface differences all sane people still believe that the truth is one in the end (whether *we* can attain to that truth or not);

which is as much as to say that there is a final objectivity which includes all the others. But most assuredly an objectivity which has forgotten the existence and importance of Subjects and their subjectivity is not likely to be the final test of truth in a universe which includes both, and where knowledge, such as we know it, involves a relation of Subject *and* Object.

Chapter 2

The Subject In Kierkegaard

Subjectivity is Truth

WE BEGIN OUR study of modern theological trends with Sören Kierkegaard (1813-55). Ever since a famous declaration of Karl Barth,[1] the Danish thinker who died almost a hundred years ago has come to be regarded by many as the great historical alternative to Schleiermacher in the parentage of modern theology. Just as philosophers used to be divided into born Platonists or Aristotelians, so it would now appear that theologians are born either Schleiermacherians or Kierkegaardians! Yet it is of Schleiermacher himself that Kierkegaard reminds us on first acquaintance, the Schleiermacher of the *Reden*, the student and translator of Plato, the *Romantiker*. Partly, of course, this is due to the literary character of Kierkegaard's approach: here is a voluminous writer on Christianity, who (though he never could have gone on to construct a *Glaubenslehre*) brought a rich and varied culture to bear upon a fundamental position, and thought no shame or hurt to set forth the central affirmation of Christianity in terms drawn as much from Greek philosophy as from the Bible. It is in terms of a contrast with the Socratic dialectic that Kierkegaard elicits the specific quality of Christian faith in the *Philosophical Fragments* (1844); but it is very evident that Socrates remains a figure precious in his own right to this wrestler with truth, no mere foil of human error against which the jewel of saving truth in Christ is set. So, too, we are warned by the best interpreters of Kierkegaard against the error of conceiving the aesthetic, the ethical and the religious "stages on life's way" as temporally successive and mutually exclusive.[2] For this man the

[1] See *The Word of God and the Word of Man*, 1928, p. 195.

[2] Lowrie's Introduction to the *Stages on Life's Way*, p. 9; quoted in Bretall *A Kierkegaard Anthology*, 1946, p. 174f.

music of a Mozart is relevant to his apprehension of what Christianity is and is not. Almost, indeed, the Christian position is seized in realization of what it is not: it is an attitude, a dialectical movement which in rising above still retains what is rejected, seen now as precious though not the pearl of great price. Here is no cheap campaign for the "de-Hellenization of Christianity." Here is no devastating repudiation of the secular, whether in science, art or philosophy; although the gospel is read, as Coleridge said of Kean's acting of Shakespeare, "by flashes of lightning" cleaving secular darkness. The reference to "dialectic" just made reminds us of Kierkegaard's debt to Hegel himself, the Hegel against whose "System" he is continually fulminating as the great contemporary misunderstanding of Christianity. The debt is positive as well as negative. "Let admirers of Hegel keep to themselves the privilege of making him out to be a bungler," he writes,[3] "an opponent will always know how to hold him in honour, as one who has willed something great, though without having achieved it." Had Hegel been content to append a footnote to his system to the effect that "the whole thing, after all, was only a 'thought-experiment,' he would have been the greatest thinker who ever lived."[4] Nevertheless, we feel sure Kierkegaard would have added, the least in the kingdom of heaven is greater than Hegel.

Moreover, the polemic against Hegel must not blind us to the great characteristic of the age which Kierkegaard shares with Hegel in philosophy and Schleiermacher in theology. All three are children of the Romantic revival and revolt against the Enlightenment. In their different ways all three are apostles of subjectivity. "The absolute is subject not substance," said the philosopher. "Religion is the intuition of the infinite, the feeling of absolute dependence," said the theologian. It remained for Kierkegaard to correct what he found false emphasis in both teachers. "The passion of the infinite is . . . subjectivity, and thus subjectivity becomes the truth."[5] Against Hegel he says, "Your absolute Subject has swallowed up the individual, and so has become indistin-

[3] *Concluding Unscientific Postscript*, E. T., 1941, p. 100n.
[4] Bretall, *op. cit.*, p. 191.
[5] *Postscript*, p. 181.

guishable from the absolute Object; subjectivity has vanished in a boundless objectivity." Against Schleiermacher we can imagine him saying, "Your subjectivity has not sufficiently allowed for the specific quality of the "object" in Christianity, where it is present to faith as paradox. Hence its true analogy is not aesthetic feeling, but an activity combined with a passivity which together constitute a passion which is the highest energizing and supreme manifestation of subjectivity."

It is no light undertaking to try to expound what Kierkegaard means by "subjectivity." This is the real theme of a large and difficult book of some 550-odd pages in its English translation, the *Concluding Unscientific Postscript to the Philosophical Fragments*. There is something amusing (usually supposed feminine!) about a postscript five and a half times as long as the document to which it is appended. The humour is intentional on the part of one of the comparatively small company of theological satirists. For the *Postscript* of 1846 is really the elaboration, discussion and (from Kierkegaard's standpoint) solution of the problem posed in the *Fragments* of two years earlier. Together both make one continuous work, the masterpiece of Kierkegaard's maturity, and intended to be his last literary production, we are told. The whole is informed by the spirit of protest against Hegel. Properly, perhaps, we ought to say "against Hegelianism"; for Hegel died in 1831, and it was against Hegel's worshippers in Danish philosophical and theological circles that Kierkegaard polemized. Still, it is mainly Hegel's own ideas which Kierkegaard attacks, with all the weapons of a dialectic as keen as the master's own, even where he is careful to protest his admiration of the teacher's purely intellectual ability. But one thing which Kierkegaard found almost completely lacking in Hegel he himself possessed in superabundance, namely, humour. It is something new in the history of theology to find discussions of humour itself, the absurd, the comic, and their opposites the tragic, pathos, irony, even madness itself, entering into the definition of the Christian position. Kierkegaard's humour enters, then, into the very titles of the two parts of the conjoint opus we are now considering. The *Philosophical Fragments or a Fragment of Philosophy* are so called in protest against the claim to systematic quality in Hegel's writings, and the implied claim to all-inclusive and final truth. The colloquial "bits" rather than the dignified "fragments," we are told, comes nearer to the meaning of the Danish *smuler*.[6] Well then, to "the System," with its comic claim to absoluteness, Kierkegaard opposes some "scraps" from his own philosophic thinking, and propounds a question which may well prick this pretentious bubble. The question, Kierkegaard undertakes to show, is posed by the very existence of the Christian religion, properly understood. "Is an historical point of departure possible for an eternal consciousness"? In the *Fragments* Kierkegaard shows how the Christian consciousness implies a dialectic opposed *toto caelo* to the Hegelian, rooted in a transcendent paradox which refuses incorporation in any "system" except its own. In the *Concluding Unscientific Postscript* to these *Fragments* he once again disclaims "system"—not merely "scientific" system, although the natural sciences are elsewhere (in the *Journals*) deflated in their pretensions—in an exposition of a central weakness in the Hegelian system, namely, that it submerges existence in abstract and pure thought, and so is enabled to present a false and unreal objectivity as truth. Against such an ideal Kierkegaard elaborates a doctrine of subjectivity as truth, a doctrine which makes sense of many spheres of experience in a manner beyond Hegel, and which opens up the possibility of understanding Christianity in a way more consonant with its own understanding of itself than that subordination to philosophy which is all that the deceptive patronage of Hegelianism can concede to the gospel. "Unscientific" the *Postscript* may be, unsystematic compared with the Hegelian exposition of the whole contents of the cosmos in an orderly evolution, paragraph by paragraph. But that is not the chief obstacle to our understanding of Kierkegaard's thesis that subjectivity is truth. It is not just that it is, as his fellow-countryman Georg Brandes said, "a new kind of philosophical book."[7] It is not that the *Fragments* is, as its own title-page describes it, "A Mimic-Pathetic-Dialectic Composition An Existential Contribution," a work "thickly interspersed with anecdote,

[6] A. Grieve, article—"Kierkegaard" in Hastings' *ERE*, vii, 698a.
[7] Swenson, Introduction to the *Fragments*, p. xxv.

humour, satire, irony and pathos in rich abundance,"[8] from which the doctrine has to be collected from here and there in the text. The real difficulty is that there is a tremendous, demonic consistency and system in the thought, and that the thought is new, forging its own categories and terminology, and pointing its own contrast with traditional expression in these realms. The victory is not to be won over Hegel by any retreat from philosophical thought to some less strenuous level. And if the thought and the terminology are neither of them so strange-seeming in these present days this is precisely owing to the rediscovery of Kierkegaard by our own times, and to the influence these have exercised upon the philosophical and theological movement broadly to be described as existentialist. "The beginning of the new apprehension of the problem of God dates from that moment in the nineteenth century when Kierkegaard, in conflict with the Hegelian philosophy, rediscovered the way back from abstract thought to the actually existing reality." Thus H. R. Mackintosh, in his *Types of Modern Theology* (1937, p. 226), quotes Karl Heim; and his own footnote on the same page declares that "Kierkegaard's criticism of the Hegelian philosophy is now widely recognized as one of the two or three really important examinations made of that system in the light of positive principles." And, like Marxist materialist determinism, Kierkegaard's thought, too, claims to "set the system upon its feet" in actuality.

It is immediately obvious that in Kierkegaard the Subject from which the much-discussed subjectivity is derived is not the mere epistemological Subject of Kant's analysis of knowledge. Kant had sought to fill out his idea of the actually existing human being by adding an "empirical ego" and a *"noumenal* ego" to the logical Subject of knowledge. Only the relations of the three aspects of the self had remained ambiguous, almost impossible of living relation, by reason of his dualistic ontological presuppositions. The empirical ego is more than a stream of consciousness, for it is the subject of feeling and will and the concrete determinations of character. How all this is possible when all its doings are subject to natural necessity, how in particular it can be

[8] Swenson, *loc. cit.*

capable of ethical decision implying freedom, these possibilities are saved or allowed for, by ascribing to the ego a
noumenal nature. But this is a metaphysical mystery and a
miracle outside the understandable world of science, needed
to make final sense of what goes on in knowledge, moral
action, aesthetic feeling. Kierkegaard stands near to Kant
in this feeling for the complete reality of the "individual
existing human being."[9] His Subject is all that and perhaps
more, the nature of whose intellectual, moral, aesthetic and
religious life is to be set forth with a far richer and more
concrete analysis than was at Kant's command. Subjectivity,
with Kierkegaard, was to include all these varied activities
and sensibilities in their actual manifestation. Meantime the
development since Kant had culminated in Hegel, whose
system was currently received as the last word in modernity
and finality by the intelligentsia of Kierkegaard's Danish and
German *milieu*. The system professed to have overcome the
abhorrent dualism of Kant in an ontological unity of thought
and being. All problems had been solved in principle, even if
the system might not have been completed down to the last
paragraph. God, man and the universe were now at last
transparent to thought. How could anyone want to object
further when everything, down to the most subtle manifestations of human subjectivity in art, ethics and religion had
been allowed for, had their appropriate and logically
necessary place allocated to them in the system? The whole
universe of thought and being had been shown to be one
dialectically developing process in the life of absolute spirit,
full honour and justice being done *inter alia* to the claims of
Christianity as the highest manifestation of the idea of religion.

Kierkegaard did want to object; in the name of "subjectivity" in general, in the name of Christian subjectivity in
particular. Everything had been betrayed to a false "objectivity"—knowledge, ethics, religion, Christianity above all,
in which Kierkegaard lived, suffered, surmounted his personal tragedy.

"Whether truth is defined more empirically as the conformity of thought and being, or more idealistically as the

[9] *Postscript,* p. 307n.

conformity of being with thought, it is, in either case, important carefully to note what is meant by being. And in formulating the answer to this question it is likewise important to take heed lest the knowing spirit be tricked into losing itself in the indeterminate, so that it fantastically becomes a something that no human being ever was or can be . . . That the knowing spirit is an existing individual spirit, and that every human being is such an entity existing for himself, is a truth I cannot too often repeat; for the fantastic neglect of this is responsible for much confusion."[10] All the errors of Hegel, according to Kierkegaard, arise in the end—or rather, in the beginning—from ignoring the fact that thought implies a thinker, a concrete, individual, existing thinker, having his being in time, i.e. in "becoming." Hegel thinks he has dealt with existence, has incorporated it in his system, has brought about the recognition of the identity of thought and being. When confronted by his critics with the brute nature of fact, its unideal quality as actual existence, did he not declare that "contingency itself is a category"? Existence steadily resists dissipation into purely ideal factors: Hegel has *not* incorporated existence into his system, contends Kierkegaard, but only the *idea* of existence. He has *not* brought becoming into thought, for all his talk of dialectical process and the self-realization of the absolute spirit in the life of finite human spirits in history. "As soon as the being which corresponds to the truth comes to be empirically concrete, the truth is put in process of becoming, and is . . . by way of anticipation the conformity of thought with being. This conformity is actually realized for God, but it is not realized for any existing spirit, who is himself existentially in the process of becoming."[11] The whole grandiose Hegelian system is one gigantic construction of abstract thought which has left out of sight the existence of the human thinker, particularly in his human quality of struggle or striving, and his possibility of being in error and not in the truth. "Ethics has been crowded out of the System."[12] "For a thinker as such it may be quite in order to think man in general; but *qua*

[10] *Postscript*, p. 169.
[11] *op. cit.*, p. 170.
[12] *ibid.*, p. 309.

existing individual, he is ethically forbidden to forget himself, or to forget that he is an existing individual."[13] "Everywhere it is decisively concluded that thought is the highest stage of human development; philosophy moves farther and farther away from contact with primitive existential impressions, and there is nothing left to explore, nothing to experience. Everything has been finished, and speculative thought has now to rubricate, classify and methodically arrange the various concepts. One does not live any more, one does not act, one does not believe; but one knows what love and faith are, and it only remains to determine their place in the System . . . there seems to me something horrible, something bewitched, in the dead insensibility by which actual life is reduced to a shadow existence."[14]

Most of the points in Kierkegaard's criticism of Hegel are in these quotations. Already the fateful new terminology of *existence* and *existential* has put in its appearance. Already we can see, if vaguely and in outline, the points he is making. But we pause to ask "Is it fair criticism of philosophy to object that it is not by itself life, of thought that it is not of itself existence"? Kierkegaard has himself seen this possible objection, however, and means more than this by his criticism of Hegel. "It is asserted again and again that thought becomes concrete" (*sc.*, by the Hegelians). "But in what sense does it become concrete? Surely not in the sense that it becomes a definite concrete something? That is to say, then, thought becomes concrete within the general determination that it remains essentially abstract; for the concrete is the existing, and existence corresponds to particularity, from which thought abstracts."[15] But Hegelianism claims to be more than abstract thought, or thought in general. It is the unity of thought and being: it is the highest realization of absolute spirit as objective spirit. It is final truth, the truth of life and existence of which religion is only the adumbration in a form of picture-thinking suitable for pupils in the primary stages of the education of mankind. This conceit is intolerable to Kierkegaard, and he labours to expose the

[13] *ibid.*, p. 307n.
[14] *ibid.*, p. 307f.
[15] *loc. cit.*

intellectual inconsistencies of its philosophic basis. As philosophy it is ridiculous in its claim to have allowed for the actualities of concrete existence, especially the actualities of the individual existing human being. Not only does he declare that "to assert the supremacy of thought is Gnosticism,"[16] he further maintains that "existence itself . . . as it is in the individual who raises the question and himself exists, keeps the two moments of thought and being apart."[17] We shall want, therefore, thought—even of an "existential" kind —to take account of and allow for the ways and places where and in which it cannot of itself be being—except being of a very special kind, i.e. an activity of actually existing, individual, human beings. We shall expect that, within its essentially unifying, connecting, synthesizing activity, it will be ready to acknowledge discontinuity where it shows itself, a different kind of being from its own. In his own way Kierkegaard is a *Lebensphilosoph* before Nietzsche, although he does not speak for preference about "life" but about "subjectivity." Through a multitude of witticisms he hangs on to the criticism that Hegel has carried the traditional absent-mindedness of the Herr Professor to the pitch of forgetting himself, the Subject of thought, in a very one-sided and abstract type of thinking at that, for all the boasted concreteness of the system. The sum of the matter is, as we have just heard, that "existence itself keeps the two moments of thought and being apart, so . . . reflection presents . . . two alternatives. For an objective reflection the truth becomes an object, something objective, and thought must be pointed away from the subject. For a subjective reflection the truth becomes a matter of appropriation, of inwardness, of subjectivity, and thought must probe more and more deeply into the subject and his subjectivity."[18] This last is still philosophizing; it is thought which does not try to turn itself into existence, but which remembers existence and that it is not itself existence—as Hegelianism is constantly tempted by its terminology to forget. It is a new kind of philosophizing. It is the way of the "subjective thinker." It is the road

[16] *op. cit.*, p. 305.
[17] *op. cit.*, p. 171.
[18] *op. cit.*, p. 171.

Kierkegaard himself must travel, urged on by all the compulsions of his being.

Over and over again Kierkegaard inveighs against the lack of *ethical* concern in Hegel. "The idea of a universal history tends to a greater systematic concentration of everything. A Sophist has said that he could carry the whole world in a nutshell, and this is what modern surveys of world history seem to realize. . . . Ethics and the ethical, as constituting the essential anchorage for all individual existence, have an indefeasible claim upon every existing individual; so indefeasible a claim that, whatever a man may accomplish in the world, even to the most astonishing of achievements, it is none the less quite dubious in its significance, unless the individual has been ethically clear when he made his choice, has ethically clarified his choice to himself. The ethical quality is jealous for its own integrity, and is quite unimpressed by the most astounding quantity."[19] This is Kierkegaard's version of the Kantian doctrine of the "good will" as the sole good without qualification, whether in the world or out of it. But whereas Kant could not succeed in bringing this doctrine into one coherent system with his epistemology —with his view of the primacy of natural science as the type of knowledge—Kierkegaard is resolute to put science and philosophy in their place within a dialectic of existence no less strenuous than those of Kant or Hegel. He goes on: "It is for this reason that ethics looks upon all world-historical knowledge with a degree of suspicion, because it may so easily become a snare, a demoralizing aesthetic diversion for the knowing subject, in so far as what does or does not have significance obeys a quantitative dialectic. As a consequence of this fact, the absolute ethical distinction between good and evil tends for the historical survey to be neutralized in the aesthetic-metaphysical determination of the great and significant, to which category the bad has equal admittance with the good. In the case of what has world-historic significance, another set of factors plays an essential rôle, factors which do not obey an ethical dialectic: accidents, circumstances, the play of forces entering into the historic totality that modifyingly incorporates the deed of the individual so

[19] *op. cit.*, p. 119f.

as to transform it into something that does not directly belong to him. . . . But Ethics regards as unethical the transition by which an individual renounces the ethical quality in order to try his fortune, longingly, wishingly, and so forth, in the quantitative and non-ethical."[20]

The intention of all this is fairly clear and understandable. The value of this exposition for the history of thought, and through thought its value for life, lies in the intellectual apparatus by which Kierkegaard attempts to make his position philosophically respectable. This consists essentially in a new doctrine of the Subject. The Subject in Kierkegaard is neither an abstract logical presupposition of knowledge and experience, nor a *noumenal* mystery inevitably conceived after the analogy of material substance. It is neither a mathematical point without surface or qualities, nor yet a block of being sculptured in metaphysical marble or psychological mind-stuff. It is a living, active, self-making, self-choosing, self-renewing energy, genuinely set in time, process and becoming, with its life in ethics, religion *and* knowledge vitally affected thereby. "The question I would ask is this: What conclusion would inevitably force itself upon Ethics, if the becoming a subject were not the highest task confronting a human being? And to what conclusion would ethics be forced? Aye, it would, of course, be driven to despair. But what does the System care about that? It is consistent enough not to include an Ethic in its systematic scheme."[21] "The task of becoming a subject": there is a new accent in philosophical language. This is in brief compass what Kierkegaard means by "subjectivity."

"First then the ethical, the task of becoming subjective, and afterwards the world-historical."[22] Whatever subjectivity may mean for Kierkegaard, it does *not* mean any and every manifestation of personal activity, still less any grubbing about in the depths of one's particular *psyche*. It is not the apotheosis of caprice or eccentricity, the cultivation of hothouse plants of thought or feeling. His ideal is not the "artistic personality," the cult of particularity at all costs. It

[20] *loc. cit.*
[21] *op. cit.*, p. 119.
[22] *op. cit.*, p. 142.

does not mean believing what one likes, doing just what one pleases, denying the grand objectivities of common humanity and the compulsions of universal truth. In the next chapter we shall speak of the place of "objectivity" in Kierkegaard's thought, as this chapter is devoted to what he means by "subjectivity"; and from our first we remember that these are poles of a relation, not opposite realities in conflict. Meanwhile we address ourselves to the fact that, according to Kierkegaard, the *ethical* is a fundamental dimension of human existence, and one which in some sense takes precedence of knowledge, scientific or philosophical. It is only "on paper," as we say, within the sphere of thought itself, that Hegelianism has achieved its much-vaunted identification of thought and being. Existence itself, reality as actuality or factuality, has eluded its grasp in several directions; and that not just in the subdivision of reality which is co-extensive with life, human life in particular. Later "Existentialism," so-called, has accustomed us somewhat overmuch to the idea that "existence" (*Existenz*) is a special potential of human activity. Take this explanation from a valuable book by Werner Brock: *"Existenz* is not to be confused with life. We remain in life from birth to death. We find life in our fellow-men, in animals and in plants as well as within ourselves . . . *Existenz* . . . is not there from birth. It is not at all, but it becomes; or rather it may become. *Existenz* is an attitude of an individual towards himself, which is called forth by such concrete situations as the necessity for choice of profession or a conflict in love, a catastrophic change in social conditions, or the imminence of one's own death. It leads immediately to sublime moments in which man gathers his whole strength to make a decision which is taken afterwards as binding upon his future life."[23] This passage is taken from a section dealing directly with Kierkegaard, and it represents his main emphasis, his view of subjectivity in its supreme exercise, the basis upon which he erects his doctrine of subjective thinking, as well as several directions in which later Existentialism has followed his lead. But his own use of "existence" is wider. The basis upon which intellectually he

[23] *An Introduction to Contemporary German Philosophy*, 1935, p. 82f.

seeks to justify subjective thinking against Hegel includes a use of "existence" in its more general sense of reality, actuality, factuality, in contrast with the various degrees of abstraction characteristic of thought in general, scientific, historical, philosophical. The dissatisfaction with the Hegelian dialectic is more strictly argued than the passage from Brock might lead one to suppose. There is no facile pleading of the reasons of the heart against the head, for example. There is a piece of strictly philosophical criticism of Hegel, which opposes to his a rival dialectic not less but perhaps more subtle than his own.

Below the level of human life and ethical decision at all, apart from all question of self-making or self-constituting choice at all, Kierkegaard points out that reality, actuality, factuality, *Existenz,* the concretely existing scheme of things is caught up in change or becoming, in process and movement, which the Hegelian system and idealist thinking generally tend to explain away, to depreciate Platonistically in favour of the eternity of thought, which is not a genuine eternity after all, but the stillness of abstraction, of timelessness. The victory which Hegel boasts of having achieved in this matter, by incorporating movement in his very system as its life-blood, is after all a victory in thought only, a win in the round of "shadow-boxing," to use one of Kierkegaard's own favourite metaphors. To Platonism in this matter Kierkegaard opposes an Aristotelianism for which he was, on his own showing, partially indebted to a contemporary German thinker, himself no mean antagonist of Hegel. Adolf Trendelenburg (1802-72), from 1833 Professor at the University of Berlin, had in his *Logische Untersuchungen* (1840) used the Aristotelian logic against the Hegelian dialect in an emphasis upon movement and multiplicity. "Movement produces multiplicity and at the same time exhibits the unity of the whole. From purposive movement everywhere are derived both the outer world of being and the inner world of thought."[24] The short section labelled *Interlude* in the *Philosophical Fragments* (pp. 59-73) of Kierkegaard is an extraordinarily condensed piece of philosophical argumentation applying the logic of becoming to the demolition of necessity

[24] Article "Trendelenburg" in *Religion in Gegenwart und Geschichte* (2nd Ed.), Heft V, 1268.

as valid of the existing world. Necessity is a category of modality and obtains only of thought. "All becoming takes place with freedom, not by necessity. Nothing that comes into being does so by virtue of a logical ground, but only through the operation of a cause. Every cause terminates in a freely operating cause."[25] Furthermore, "everything that has come into being is *eo ipso* historical" and "viewed in this light . . . nature has a history."[26] The upshot of all this is hammered home in the *Postscript* where it is declared "(A), a logical system is possible; (B), an existential system is impossible."[27] Kierkegaard does not here dwell further upon the fact that even nature has a history, beyond pointing out that the natural sciences are "abstract," and that their "necessity" belongs to them as "thought-constructions" not as "existence." Only "immediate sensation and immediate cognition cannot deceive."[28] All history, including the history of nature, as apprehension of the past, is "approximation knowledge," since "as compared with the immediate, becoming has an elusiveness by which even the most dependable fact is rendered doubtful."[29] For nature and history in their quality of becoming the organ appropriate to the uncertainty inherent in becoming is belief, or, more strongly *faith*. "Faith believes what it does not see; it does not believe that the star is there, for that it sees, but it does believe that the star has come into being . . . The "what" of a happening may be known immediately, but by no means can it be known immediately that it has happened. Nor can it be known immediately that it happens, not even if it happens, as we say, in front of our very noses. The elusiveness pertaining to an event consists in its having happened, in which fact lies the transition from nothing, from non-being, and from the manifold possible "how."[30]

If existence displays this unsystematic, this a-logical character, even at the level of nature; if knowledge even here involves a "leap" in arriving at belief; how much less

[25] *Fragments*, p. 61f.
[26] *loc. cit.*
[27] *Postscript*, p. 99.
[28] *Fragments*, p. 66.
[29] *loc. cit.*
[30] *op. cit.*, p. 67.

shall we expect human nature to fit into a thought-project which wins its victories by the elimination of movement, of real becoming, of self-making? If the thinking Subject makes "leaps," jumps over discontinuities in arriving at science and history; if there is qualitative as well as quantitative distinction in the knowledge of the actual; how shall we expect the ethical Subject to find the truth about itself reflected in a "system" which has no place for "the task of *becoming* a subject," since the real is already the rational, and all qualitative difference and distinction have been submerged in a logic of mediation and identity?

"From the poetic and intellectual standpoint, possibility is higher than reality, the aesthetic and the intellectual being disinterested. There is only one interest, the interest in existence; disinterestedness is therefore an expression for indifference to reality. . . . That the content of my thought exists in the conceptual sense needs no proof . . . since it is proved by my thinking it. But as soon as I proceed to impose a teleology upon my thought, and bring it into relation with something else, interest begins to play a rôle in the matter. The instant this happens the ethical is present, and absolves me from any further responsibility in proving my own existence. It forbids me to draw a conclusion that is ethically deceitful and metaphysically unclear, by imposing upon me the duty of existing. . . . Ethically regarded, reality is higher than possibility. The ethical proposes to do away with the disinterestedness of the possible, by making existence the infinite interest. . . . The aesthetic and intellectual principle is that no reality is thought or understood until its *esse* has been resolved into its *posse*. The ethical principle is that no possibility is understood until its *posse* has really become an *esse*. . . . The ethical reality of the individual is the only reality."[31]

These quotations from consecutive pages of a single section of the *Postscript* show what Kierkegaard means by the ethical, and how he proposes to make room for it intellectually by annihilating the presumption of Hegelianism systematically to articulate all reality. They also illustrate what he means by subjectivity. The "infinite interest in existence," which is the sphere of the ethical, requires that the

[31] *Postscript*, pp. 282-291.

Subject translates its own *posse* into *esse*, and that "the task of becoming a subject" is laid upon it by its very nature as ideality existing in time and history. The Subject does not just exist; it exists for itself, as an idea or ideal of itself, which it ever and again has to translate from possibility into actuality, in a kind of ever renewed self-creation. Every moment, not just once in every five or six centuries, this Phoenix dies and is reborn. Subjective thinking is therefore "infinitely interested" thinking, in this specialized Kierkegaardian sense. Once again, this does not mean that we think what and as we like. It means that, for Subjects, who exist in time and becoming, and for whom the ethical is a dimension of reality, the truth is something which they bring to pass, is a quality of their own being or existence. Not any and every exercise of the Subject's will in knowledge or action is "in the truth." Error is real—in particular, the real is not necessarily the ethical rational. Although Kierkegaard accuses the system of lack of ethical interest he does not erect a rival system of ethics, for the only ethics in which he is interested are the ethics of the Christian religion. Before we go on to discuss what Kierkegaard's principle that "subjectivity is truth" means in the sphere of religion, however, we sum up his "existential" criticism of Hegelianism in two positions, corresponding to the two levels at which he finds the system deficient in a sense of "existence," his usage here being wider than that of some later Existentialism.

Firstly: Kierkegaard is not reproaching Hegel for any fault in "thought" (especially philosophical thought) that it is not itself "being" (except the peculiar kind of being which we may designate "ideality"). Kierkegaard does complain that Hegelianism has not allowed for the real reason why thought cannot be being, i.e. that at the level of existence as actuality, factuality, reality in time and becoming, there is a distinction between the "what" and the "how" or "that," such that even nature has a history. Thought can be systematized: it is in any case a series of still-life pictures from the film of reality, abstractions and constructions, between whose component parts the modal category of necessity can, in accordance with the state of knowledge in that department, be asserted. By thinking that it has allowed for being and movement, the system has confused itself into the belief that it has overcome the dualism between being and thought, which existence itself—even at this lowest, widest level—keeps apart.

Secondly: at the ethical level, Hegel has not allowed for the fact that the Subject here does not just or simply "exist," but makes its own existence. Self-making refuses systematization, for it implies freedom: necessity here is at least of a different kind than that in which the system deals. This consideration must make a vast difference to the resultant picture of reality. It may strike a mortal blow at any system claiming omniscience, professing to exhibit the articulation of the dialectical movement of all existence, down to the very last paragraph of the story.

What, then, does the principle that "subjectivity is truth" mean within the sphere of religion? We preface what is here said with the warning that subjectivity in Kierkegaard is not the negation of objectivity. In the next chapter we shall be dealing with the nature and the place of the Object in his construction of Christian thinking; and then we shall see that the principle is very far indeed from meaning that in religious faith we believe what we want to believe or because we want to believe, because it is comforting to believe, because it suits (or does not suit!) our psychological make-up to believe, or even that we make an entirely self-originated choice of believing in some particular set of religious realities. These things said, we go on to the statement that for Kierkegaard subjectivity finds its highest exercise in Christian faith, and proceed to examine what this means.

In Christian faith, specifically; not in religious belief in general. True, anything that Kierkegaard would be prepared to call real religious belief and practice anywhere would be, would require to be, an exercise in subjectivity. Few things in Kierkegaard are more impressive and even moving than his devotion to the figure of Socrates. It is from a consideration of the procedure of Socrates in the Platonic dialogues, particularly the *Meno,* that the argument of the *Philosophical Fragments* sets out to establish the particularity of the Christian view of faith. There are more references—by name, at least—to Socrates than to Hegel in the *Concluding Scientific Postscript*. From the latter work we take this summary statement. "The Socratic secret, which must be preserved in Christianity, unless the latter is to be an infinite backward step, and which in Christianity receives an intensification, by means of a more profound inwardness which makes it infinite, is that the movement of the spirit is inward, that the truth is the subject's transformation in himself."[32] What specially attracted Kierkegaard to Socrates was not only the modesty of the man who professed to know nothing except his own ignorance (in contrast to the implied claim to omniscience in Hegel), but precisely Socrates' complete personal involvement in the quest for truth. Truth is a matter in which the Subject is totally interested, not completely disinterested. And, like the Christ himself, Socrates was interested to the point of giving himself in life and death in fidelity to this vocation. The historical details of the polemic which Kierkegaard waged against the contemporary Church in Denmark are outside our scope. But not so the main motive of the attack; which is a highly personal version of the ancient thesis that Christianity is nothing if it is not first and last a form of spirituality. It is not an institutional status into which we can be born, or admitted by baptism *ex opere operato*. It is not an orthodoxy to which we can subscribe, still less a doctrine which philosophy can take under its wing and render more or less respectable—as Hegelianism had done in the highest and widest circles in the Denmark of Kierkegaard's time. It is inwardness, appropriation, struggle, despair, fear and trembling, ultimately faith—an attitude which is the beginning and end alike of this cycle, ever renewed, never complete, expressing itself outwardly and ethically, yet never confusing itself with this expression, precisely because it is radical inwardness, or, in Kierkegaard's terminology, subjectivity. Throughout, Kierkegaard refuses or hesitates to call himself or his thought by the definite name of Christian, even so much seeming to him externalization, objectification of what should to the end remain inwardness. Thus his theses are advanced as "thought-projects" (at least in the pseudonymous works)— this is how Christianity would describe itself or explain itself, were he entitled to speak for Christianity. Socrates could give

[32] *op. cit.*, p. 37f.

Christians lessons both in modesty and strenuousness towards the truth; for he was one of the first and greatest of subjective thinkers.

Nevertheless, Christianity is *toto caelo* different and removed from the Socratic version of subjectivity; for Socrates thought that "at bottom every human being is in possession of the Truth."[33] Knowledge is recollection, and the *Meno* shows Socrates eliciting by simple questioning some Euclidean theorems from a slave boy who has never studied geometry. The truths of morality, individual and social, similarly yield themselves to the dialectical process of question and answer, such as is set forth in the *Republic* of Plato. So far as the truth may be known men already know it, have learned it here or in a previous existence—know it *in posse*. The modern version of this position is that knowledge is a systematic totality of elements mutually involving and implying each other, truth being immanent in the whole in such a fashion that the search can proceed from knowledge of any one element to any and ultimately all the others. We are in the truth and the truth is in us: we need merely unwind the clue to come at last to the citadel. We may indeed require some assistance on the road, as the slave boy in the *Meno* needed the prompting leading questions of Socrates to arrive at the correct geometrical conclusions. But Socrates himself was no part of the conclusion. The teacher vanished when the final truth appeared. Time is irrelevant in the end, for truth is eternal; the historical accidents of its discovery and acquisition do not enter into its essence or composition. *In posse* reason is always in possession of the whole truth. Realism as well as idealism—nay! even scepticism—are all equally agreed on this immanentist, unhistorical, eternal view of the nature of truth.

It so happens that there is an alternative, a rival view, in the field. "Is an historical point of departure possible for an eternal consciousness; how can such a point of departure have any other than a mere historical interest; is it possible to base an eternal happiness upon historical knowledge"? This is the possibility which Kierkegaard proposes to discuss in the *Philosophical Fragments or a Fragment of Philosophy*. To

[33] *Fragments*, p. 9.

discuss philosophically, let it be noted, even although Socrates may think "this all amounts to . . . scrapings and parings of systematic thought . . . divided into bits."[34] And where has this rival view turned up from? It is, contends Kierkegaard with all the energy of his very life-blood, the heart of the Christian gospel, so distorted and misrepresented in the current Hegelian modes of thought, to whose dialectic of immanence he opposes a dialectic of revelation and transcendence. Here is truth which can only be appropriated existentially in a supreme exercise of subjectivity, corresponding to the scandal which the Christian message offers to reason in the paradox of its central affirmation: the eternal entered time in an historical person, bringing truth and salvation in Jesus Christ, to those who believe or have faith in Him. If Jesus Christ is not just another Teacher, Himself ultimately irrelevant to the truth of the message He proclaimed; if He is, in the historical event of His appearance on earth, Himself the message which faith appropriates; then He is the coming of truth to us, not our coming to the truth. Furthermore, this involves that we are not, that human reason is not, as such, in the truth, but in error or untruth. The ethical will is not in process of achieving the good: it is itself in sin. The beggar maiden who marries the king in this fable or fairy-tale—for such it must appear to them that are without—does so because the incredible is true, the fairytale or fable has unbelievably become fact. If the eternity of truth is not spread immanently over the whole process of becoming, but entered the process at a particular point in historical time, then this is a qualitatively different kind of eternity which discounts all abstract truth, scientific or philosophical, all "approximation knowledge" of history, even "sacred history"; for the eternal consciousness based upon the historical point of departure of the incarnation of God in the man Christ Jesus eighteen hundred-odd years ago before Kierkegaard wrote is not objective historical knowledge. The eternal consciousness which is salvation is a subjective appropriation by faith of this paradox, and so is the "highest passion in the sphere of human subjectivity."[35] It is the

[34] *Postscript*, p. 2.
[35] *Postscript*, p. 118.

"highest passion" because there is no approach to it along any immanental, objective ground; because it is response going against the whole dialectic of conviction in other spheres, putting the whole process of thinking in reverse. There is no ground for adhering to the "paradox," except that it presents itself as the truth. The "leap" which we have heard of elsewhere in the matter of coming to a decision concerning becoming is here widened to a jump across an abyss. Doubtless there are aspects of life and experience which prepare and may predispose us to make such a leap. But nowhere else are we asked to jump out of and over ourselves in this fashion. "To preserve myself in faith I must constantly be intent upon holding fast the objective uncertainty, so as to remain out upon the deep, over seventy thousand fathoms of water."[36] "Faith is precisely the contradiction between the infinite passion of the individual's inwardness and the objective uncertainty."[37] Faith is subjectivity in its highest exercise, not because it has no object, but because its object is the paradox that "the Eternal came into being at a definite moment in time as an individual man."[38]

[36] *Postscript*, p. 182.
[37] *loc. cit.*
[38] *op. cit.*, p. 512.

Chapter 3

The Object In Kierkegaard

Paradox, Faith and History

FROM CONSIDERATION OF what subjectivity meant for Kierke-gaard we turn now to the status of the Object in his system (if he will pardon us the word!) and what is his conception of objectivity. Kierkegaard was too good a philosopher to forget that there can never be a Subject without an Object, that the two are correlative terms. At no point in his exposi-tion is there the slightest suggestion of the loom of subjectivity running on with no yarn feeding from the bobbins of objectivity. The activity of the Subject in arriving at truth is not the productivity of the spider's spinning a web out of its own substance. Subjectivity is neither intellectual nor ethical solipsism. His is not the Identity Philosophy of a Schelling in which the Subject posits the Object, the ego produces the non-ego, spirit objectifies itself in matter in a polarity which constitutes nature. From all such apotheosis of self the man who wished for his tombstone the simple epitaph "the individual" is removed by the whole pathos of his life and work. His personal destiny may have isolated Kierke-gaard from the world and his fellows in an interior life of tremendous stress and strain; although he was a man with many friends and well enough off materially to indulge his sociability. But this "genius in a market town"[1] was neither an aesthete in an ivory tower nor a regarder of the shadows of the world in a mirror. In a life devoid of striking outward incident Kierkegaard was all the while profoundly involved in the world and committed to existence. The Object retained sufficient hold upon him and he upon it to save his intense intellectual life from the final madness of a Nietzsche; although he himself says he came near to this, having "from

[1] I owe the phrase to H. J. Blackham's *Six Existentialist Thinkers*, 1951, p. 1.

earliest years . . . been nailed fast to some suffering or other . . . which must have its deeper roots in a disproportion between soul and body."[2] Finally, the division of his literary activity into works appearing under various pseudonyms and others over his own name, the former broadly speaking philosophical and the latter avowedly written from the Christian standpoint, should not blind us to the fact that in intention Kierkegaard is explicating and vindicating the peculiar dialectic of the Christian religion all the time. On the penultimate page of the *Philosophical Fragments*[3] he confesses this Christian origin and reference of the positions hypothetically advanced therein as a "thought-project." "With respect to your many animadversions, all pointing to my having introduced borrowed expressions in the course of my exposition. That such is the case I do not deny, nor will I now conceal from you that it was done purposely, and that in the next section of this piece, if ever I write such a section, it is my intention to call the whole by its right name, and to clothe the problem in its historical costume . . . what the historical costume of the following section will be is not difficult to see. It is well known that Christianity is the only historical phenomenon which in spite of the historical, nay precisely by means of the historical, has offered itself to the individual as a point of departure for his eternal consciousness, has assumed to interest him in another sense than the merely historical, has proposed to base his eternal happiness on his relationship to something historical. No system of philosophy, addressing itself solely to the thought, no mythology, addressing itself solely to the imagination, no historical knowledge, addressing itself to the memory, has ever had this idea: of which it may be said . . . that it did not arise in the heart of any man. But this is something I have to a certain extent wished to forget, and, making use of the unlimited freedom of an hypothesis, have assumed that the whole was a curious conceit of my own; which I did not wish to abandon, however, until I had thought it through." The "borrowed expressions" just referred to were, of course, such passages in the *Fragments* as the fable of the king who loved a beggar maid, and condescended to such disguise as would not confound her with his glory—which recalls New Testament language concerning the incarnate Son of God's "taking the form of a servant"—and the elaborate exposition of how the "disciples at second-hand" have no advantage over the "contemporary disciple" of the divine Teacher, but rather are the less liable to be confused in the fundamental attitude of faith by merely historical accidents of His teaching and appearing—all of which is a transparent paraphrase of the word of Christ, in the Fourth Gospel: "It is expedient for you that I go away." The "next section" to the *Fragments*, which here Kierkegaard promises provisionally, is, of course, the tremendous *Postscript*, which was published two years later. Here the Christian reference is explicit throughout; and here, too, Kierkegaard acknowledges the authorship of the pseudonymous works, so bringing them into the category of Christian exposition and apologetic.

It cannot be too much emphasized that Kierkegaard's argumentation is not an attempt to deduce the truth of the Christian religion from a formal analysis of the features of the human situation, to show that the dialectic of existence drives man inevitably towards a theistic conclusion, or a readiness to accept the Christian doctrine of sin and salvation. The Christian conclusion of the argument is not derived from an analysis or dialectic of any kind: in Kierkegaard it is presupposed. What he is really doing in the two major works we have been considering could hardly be better expressed than in the words of a recent German expositor. In *Die Existenzdialektik von Sören Kierkegaard,* 1950, at the beginning of a "Second interim report upon the dialectical method" Hermann Diem writes: "We saw how Kierkegaard in the *Philosophical Fragments* made the fact of revelation a theme of the dialectic of existence. He introduced there this fact as a pure "thought-experiment," in the meantime without historical costume, which latter he proceeded to add in the *Unscientific Postscript.* In this manner he elaborated the distinctively Christian existential categories, in contrast with the understanding of existence characteristic of ethical and religious immanence. How did he arrive at this fact, however?

Naturally he took it from the Christian tradition, and he made use extensively of the dogmatic determinations of Church doctrine in unfolding the problems thereupon arising. . . . He in no way repudiates the task of dogmatics, but himself makes use of the constructions of ecclesiastical doctrine. . . . But he himself did not see his own task in dogmatic work."[4]

Now this feature of Kierkegaard's work is itself of the utmost importance. Modern Existentialism, which derives historically from a discovery of Kierkegaard, which uses his terminology and concepts in liberal measure, yet arrives at very various conclusions in the hands of its different exponents. It is (at least, so they themselves say!) non-theistic in Heidegger and atheistic in Sartre, ambiguous in its religious implications in Jaspers, theistic and Christian (even Roman Catholic, of a sort!) in Gabriel Marcel. Existentialism appears to stand for a methodology sufficiently homogeneous in these different thinkers to warrant an identical name. But the methodology does not commit in advance to a religious conclusion. Where this does emerge it has the appearance of resulting from the existentialist attitude as its major premise. If this is to be taken as integral to Existentialism, then honesty compels us to say of Kierkegaard that "the father of Existentialism" is not an existentialist. There is, on his view, no logic of the human situation, no dialectic of existence any more than any dialectic of thought, which necessarily yields or even yields on a balance of probabilities the Christian view of man, the world, and God. Kierkegaard would have repudiated such a suggestion with horror as a new assertion of immanence. This is precisely what he means by "the paradox" of Christianity, that "it never entered into the heart of man to imagine." To concede its happening is to break with all the categories of thought and life other than those which the paradox itself proceeds to produce by a new creation. That "the Deity, the Eternal, came into being at a definite moment in time as an individual man"[5] is not conceivable apart from the Church's proclamation that it did happen in Jesus Christ. It remains inconceivable, a stumbling-

[4] op. cit., p. 77.
[5] Postscript, p. 512.

block to reason, in the minds of those who adhere to it as the very basis of their eternal happiness by faith, the infinite passion of subjectivity, which brings with it the entirely new set of existential categories of sin, guilt, forgiveness and reconciliation, in which this salvation is appropriated. And while faith continues to hang on for very life to an objective uncertainty, this infinite passion of subjectivity is yet completely motivated by an Object, by something which it did not produce, by something which in the end produces the subjectivity. Kierkegaard's service to Christianity is not a "transcendental deduction" of the categories of its thought and life from any antecedent necessities either of thought or life. It is rather to show that the possibilities and the realities here have not been truly set forth in the Hegelian account of them, nor can they be in any similar dialectic of immanence. Morever, when we recollect that reality is existence as well as idea we can leave a place within reason in the larger sense for the impossible possibility of Christianity. We could not anticipate the gospel. But we are not compelled to deny it, once it has been announced, because reason otherwise can make nothing of it.

We must now attempt a closer definition of the Object of Christian saving faith, according to Kierkegaard. Nothing is commoner than to speak of the *historical* character of this Object as giving the specific note of the Christian religion. Kierkegaard shares this language, but it is all-important to attend to his own explanation of what he means by it. Partly this emphasis derives from the awakening sense of the historical displayed by the late eighteenth century generally. German romanticism in Herder had become conscious of the folk origins of national cultures, and already in a wider reference the tide was turning against the Enlightenment's indifference to history as the seed-bed of ideas. Kierkegaard makes extensive use of another figure in this development, G. E. Lessing, who had been fruitfully aware of the importance of history for Christianity. In the account of this thinker in the eighteenth-century "prehistory" to his most illuminating story of Protestant theology in the nineteenth[6]

[6] *Die protestantische Theologie im 19 Jahrhundert*, 1947, p. 208ff.

Karl Barth undertakes to show (and seems to me to succeed) that the famous dictum of Lessing, so often quoted, "Accidental truths of history can never yield proof of necessary truths of reason," was not intended by its author to derogate from the importance of the former in the spiritual life of man. Rather Lessing wished to call attention to the differences in the sources of conviction in the two classes of truth. History is evidence, not demonstration, and certainly decreases with each step in time away from the original happenings, which, being factual are accidental from the standpoint of logic. History is, as Kierkegaard calls it, "approximation knowledge." Therefore, argues Lessing, the convictions upon which life proceeds are based upon some other sort of authentication. He speaks about "feeling," "experience," "the heart," "the beatific beat of the electric spark," as what he understands by "the demonstration of the spirit and of power"—the title of the work from which the dictum under discussion is taken.[7] Kierkegaard was before Barth in borrowing assistance for Christian apologetic from Lessing on this very point. In the *Postscript* he accepts the help of Lessing in so far as the latter points to the place of the historical in Christianity, the importance of the Bible, miracle, prophecy, in calling forth faith. In terms almost of Lessing's contrast of the sources of vital conviction with the balancing of historical evidence Kierkegaard underlines with tremendous emphasis the point that Christianity proposes to treat a matter of history in a way that goes beyond the nature of historical evidence as such when it bases the eternal happiness of an individual in the nineteenth century on the tradition of something that happened in the first century. From Lessing Kierkegaard takes the expression that faith involves a *leap*. But there is a difference in the nature of the leap of saving faith as conceived by Kierkegaard and Lessing. For Lessing the leap is from probability to conviction, from a tradition concerning long-past events, for which more or less evidence can be adduced, to a certainty which might have been ours had we been contemporaries of the events in question. The "ugly broad ditch" of which Lessing speaks derives from the difference between contemporaneity and

[7] K. Barth, *op. cit.*, p. 226.

non-contemporaneity; between seeing a thing happen with our own eyes and under our very own noses, and hearing tell of it from eye-witnesses at first or second-hand; and this last on oral or written testimony, the reliability of which diminishes in inverse ratio to the distance in time down through the centuries. For Kierkegaard, on the other hand, the leap is of a different kind; of a kind more analogous though not identical with Lessing's distinction between historical evidence as such and the grounds on which one leaps to a vital conclusion, a principle upon which one bases one's life and conduct. This last is an example of the Aristotelian *metabasis eis allo genos*. The historical happening upon which Christianity proposes to base the individual's eternal happiness is something in respect of which there is in the end no distinction between the privilege of contemporary and non-contemporary witness, and no advantage on the side of the eye-witness. For, although it happens in history, it is an eternal fact of a unique order with no historical parallels: it is the coming of God, the Deity, the Eternal, into being at a definite moment in time as an individual man. This is something that can happen under our very noses and our eyes may not see it. In Jesus Christ God came in the form of a servant, in an *incognito* necessitated by the case that no man can see God and live. It is absolutely essential that the incarnation should be historical fact, an historical fact, both event and process; only thus can the circle of immanence be broken and the specific categories of Christianity rendered existentially possible and for faith necessary, their supremacy in the sphere of salvation be established. An *historical* fact, and *an* historical fact; but *an* historical fact in the sense of the unique particularity of its happening, not in the sense of its being one of a class of such happenings in history, recognizable by the usual processes by which we establish the occurrence of happenings in history. The incarnation is both formally and materially unique in the character of its historical happening, in a way that ultimately baffles history and eludes history. Not only its "that" and its "how" but the very "what" of this historical happening are inaccessible to the purely historical point of view. So much seems required to be said of Kierkegaard's position, whatever the difficulties in which it may involve him and us. At all events, it is the end of historical immanence. It is not a truth of history we come to find and are compelled by the evidence to acknowledge as either certain or most highly probable. This would mean once more that the truth would be in us and we in the truth when we came to recognize it, not that the truth came among us to make us free. Hence "it is clear," Kierkegaard says, "that the *Fragments* really oppose Lessing, in so far as he has posited an advantage on the side of contemporaneity. It is in the denial of this advantage that the real dialectical problem lies."[8] What then is the dialectic of the leap of faith in Kierkegaard?

"At the outset let us make it clear that the question of an historical point of departure arises even for a contemporary disciple," i.e. for one who recognized in Jesus during His lifetime the entrance of the eternal into time.[9] How little (and how much!) the historical as such is to be identified with the Object of Christian faith, however, is apparent when we reflect, says Kierkegaard, that on one point—an all-important point, it would appear on Kierkegaard's view, from his singling it out for mention—"with respect to the Teacher's birth, he [i.e. the contemporary disciple] will be in the same position as the disciple at second-hand; if we urge absolute historical precision there will be only one human being who is fully informed, namely, the woman of whom he permitted himself to be born."[10] Not only were there contemporaries of Jesus who did not believe in His divine origin and significance; those who did become His disciples did so not in virtue of the fullest historical acquaintance with Him and His mission. "A knowledge of all the circumstances with the reliability of an eye-witness, does not make an eye-witness a disciple."[11] The "historical phenomenon" of the appearance of God in Jesus "proposes to interest him [i.e. the contemporary disciple] in another sense than the merely historical, presenting itself to him as a condition for his eternal happiness. If . . . not . . . then . . . the Teacher is not

[8] *Postscript*, p. 89n.
[9] *Fragments*, p. 47.
[10] *Fragments*, p. 47.
[11] *op. cit.*, p. 48.

God but only a Socrates."[12] The fullest and most detailed information about the movements of Jesus, collected by an observer who "reduced his hours of sleep to a minimum" and followed the Teacher about "more closely than the pilot-fish the shark" would still be separated from believing faith by the whole breadth of "the leap." A collection of the discourse and teaching of Jesus compiled by one who "kept a hundred assistants watching for every syllable, so that nothing should be lost" might still be making use of the Teacher "as an occasion by which he came to an understanding of himself, and . . . be able to forget the Teacher."[13] The difference between the Socratic and the Christian positions is that in the latter "the object of faith is not the *teaching* but the *Teacher.* The Socratic principle is that the learner, being himself in the truth and in possession of the condition, can thrust the teacher aside . . . But faith must steadily hold to the Teacher . . . That God has once for all given man the requisite condition is the eternal Socratic presupposition, which comes into no hostile collision with time, but is incommensurable with the temporal and its determinations. The contradiction of our hypothesis is that man receives the condition in the "moment," the same condition which as being requisite for the understanding of the eternal Truth is *eo ipso* an eternal condition . . . otherwise we stand at the Socratic principle of Recollection."[14] All this means that, in the end, "there is no disciple at second-hand. The first and the last are essentially on the same plane, only that a later generation finds its occasion in the testimony of a contemporary, while the contemporary finds this occasion in its own contemporaneity."[15] The operative testimony of the contemporary generation can be very briefly expressed. "If the contemporary generation had left behind them but these words: "We have believed that in such and such a year God appeared among us in the humble form of a servant, that he lived and taught in our community, and finally died" it would be more than enough . . . this little advertisement, this *nota bene* on a page of

[12] *op. cit.*, p. 47.
[13] *op. cit.*, p. 48.
[14] *op. cit.*, p. 50.
[15] *op. cit.*, p. 88.

universal history would be sufficient to afford an occasion for a successor, and the most voluminous account can in all eternity do nothing more."[16]

We now have fairly before us the essentials of Kierkegaard's view of the relation of Christian faith to history. We now pause to ask: is this what Christianity has usually meant when it describes itself as an historical religion? This leaves the question open as to whether the traditional view is or is not itself adequate or "correct." What becomes, on such a view, of the long *preparatio evangelica* in the history of Israel as recorded in the Old Testament, in prophets, lawgivers and psalmists? Has the detail of this development no relevance to the content of revelation? Or in affirming so do we reintroduce an immanentist idea of "the temporal and its determinations"? It is certainly to give a positive value to these, different from the indifference to history shown by the Socratic principle, but surely also an alternative to the Kierkegaardian evaluation of time! Does Kierkegaard really give a positive value to the temporal? Is not his doctrine of the "moment" in reality a depreciation of time? Revelation is concentrated "historically" in the sole phenomenon of the appearance of God in the individual man Jesus at a particular point in the time-process; and this "eternal fact" is appropriated by faith in corresponding "moments" down through the believing ages, when subjectivity penetrates the merely historical phenomenon of Jesus to the eternal fact of which it is the incognito. May we not apply to such a view a term borrowed from latter-day Existentialism and say that only the subjective appropriation of this salvation constitutes "real history"? If this is not to dismiss most of history as "bunk" with Mr. Henry Ford, it is to view it as "cinders" with T. E. Hulme in his *Speculations.*[17] Here we are not concerned to ask whether this may not after all be the "true" view of history, but only how it accords with Christianity's understanding of itself. Is it the view presupposed in the concern of the sub-apostolic age to preserve the tradition of the words and deeds of Jesus in the Synoptic Gospels—even if we give the fullest scope to the modern awareness of how much these are

[16] *op. cit.,* p. 87.
[17] *Speculations,* 1936, p. 217ff.

themselves the product or testimony of believing faith? We are told by Kierkegaard that the Teacher, not the teaching, is the revelation, the object of faith. Is this an antithesis that adequately reflects the gospel tradition? Is it a matter of *no* account towards the grounding of faith, what manner of man Jesus was, what He said and did, how He lived and died? Is faith only concerned with the "that" of Jesus' appearance on earth, and not at all with the "what" of that manifestation? Does only one feature of the Jesus-event matter to faith, namely, that Jesus was God incarnate in the form of a servant? Nay! in that very formula is there not an intermingling of the "that" with the "what"? Twice over, perhaps? Is not to say "Jesus is the appearing of God as an individual man at a particular point in time" to state *that* an historical event occurred and *what* this event was, i.e. the incarnation of God? This last is an "eternal fact," incommensurate with "history." This is "the paradox." But to go on to add "in the form of a servant" is not merely to repeat the mystery of the appearing in flesh as a man at one point in time and history. It is to fill out the otherwise featureless "eternal fact" with concrete historical detail derived from the story of Jesus' days on earth, from the outward and inward mission and message of Jesus. True, in Kierkegaard, "the form of a servant" is presented as a somewhat negative feature of the revelation in Jesus (we are speaking of the logic and argument of the conjoint opus of the *Fragments* and the *Postscript,* whatever may be the case with the rest of his works). "In order that he may have the power to give the condition the Teacher must be God; in order that he may be able to put the learner in possession of it he must be Man."[18] "Must be Man"! Any kind of man? I find one concession on Kierkegaard's part to the view that "the form of a servant" means more than "within the formal limits and conditions of humanity, of human nature." "That He was a servant means then only that He was a common man, humble and lowly, not to be distinguished from the multitude of men either by soft raiment or other earthly advantages. . . . But though in these ways resembling common men, His thoughts and cares are not like those which fill the minds of

[18] *Fragments,* p. 50.

men in general. He goes His way indifferent to the distribution and division of earthly goods . . . He is without anxiety for His daily bread . . . He does not trouble Himself about house or home . . . He is not bound to any woman, so as to be charmed by her and desirous of pleasing her. He seeks one thing only, the love of the disciple."[19] This last phrase is surely most significant, as is the whole paragraph. Here the "form of a servant" takes on the concrete details of the gospel picture of Jesus; and here is a hint that faith may be called forth by love answering to divine condescension. But lowliness and condescension can only have been known as such against some sort of perception that Jesus was God's saving presence among men. The divine "incognito" must not have been so complete as to be impenetrable; otherwise its purpose would have been lost. There must have been some indication, perhaps even some explicit claim on His part, that the Teacher was God—Kierkegaard does not shirk the forthright formula. In all these positions we are presented with fresh problems in the relation of faith to history in the gospel, which necessitate further exposition of Kierkegaard's statements.

"God did not assume the form of a servant to make a mockery of men; hence it cannot be His intention to pass through the world in such a manner that no human being becomes aware of His presence. He will doubtless give some sort of a sign, though every understanding resting upon an accommodation is essentially without value for one who does not receive the condition; for which reason he yields to the necessity only unwillingly. Such a sign, when given, is as capable of repelling the learner as of drawing him nearer. He humbled Himself and took upon Him the form of a servant, but . . . not . . . a servant in some private employment, attending to His tasks without in any manner making Himself known, either to His master or to his fellow-servants —such a measure of wrath we dare not ascribe to God." Upon this follows[20] the passage already quoted in which the unworldliness of Jesus' actual life among men is described. "This lofty absorption in His mission will of itself suffice to

[19] *op. cit.,* p. 45.
[20] *Fragments,* p. 45f.

attract the attention of the multitude, among whom the learner will doubtless be found . . . Let us now picture God going about in the city of His appearance . . . To make His teaching known is the sole necessity of His life; it is His meat and drink."[21] There is a curious reluctance on Kierkegaard's part to say in so many words what this teaching is! But he continues: "God's appearance has now become the news of the day, in the market place, in the homes of the people, in the council chamber, in the ruler's palace. It gives the occasion for much foolish and idle talk, perhaps also for some earnest reflection. But for the learner the news of the day is not an occasion for something else, not even an occasion for the acquirement in Socratic sincerity of a deeper and fuller self-knowledge; for the learner it is the eternal, the beginning of eternity. The news of the day the beginning of eternity! If God had permitted Himself to be born in an inn, wrapped in swaddling clothes and laid in a manger, could the contradiction have been greater than that the news of the day should be the swaddling clothes of eternity! . . . Unless God grants the condition which makes it possible to understand this, how is it to be supposed that the learner will be able to discover it!"[22] "God's appearance the news of the day": this formula presupposes not just that God has entered time and history in Jesus as a fact which might never have been known, but that someone somehow *has* known and reported it, and the rumour is now widespread and is believed for gospel truth (indeed!) by certain individuals. Is it the guess or intuition of the spiritually minded, i.e. "divination" in Rudolf Otto's sense of the word? That would be on Kierkegaard's terms a lapse back into immanence: "flesh and blood would have revealed it" after all. It is impossible to doubt that Kierkegaard holds rather to an explicit self-witness of Jesus to His divine origin and significance such as is unambiguous only in the pages of the Fourth Gospel, of which the *Philosophical Fragments,* so often suggest a paraphrase. There is an explicit claim; there is also a life consonant with the claim, sufficiently different from the common life of humanity to arouse attention. But are

[21] *loc. cit.*
[22] *ibid.*

not those elements of history, in the common acceptance of the terms? They belong to the picture of Jesus which later came to be termed "the historical Jesus" or "the Jesus of history." Evidently Kierkegaard allows them some weight, in such passages as we have quoted, in determining the venture of faith. But over against this is set another, a completely unhistorical account of the origin of faith as a miracle happening in the "moment," with no immanent implications. The genesis of faith in individual believers occurs at certain points in chronological time; it is occasioned by an event which took place at a definite date in universal history, whereof the contemporary belief that it took place has been transmitted to later generations, by a written and institutional record. But here history is only the locus of the original event and of contemporary and later belief. The content of history has no place in faith, in spite of what has just been quoted from Kierkegaard, for its Object is an "eternal fact," the entrance of God into history at a point of time and place. The spark which kindles faith is in the end miracle outside history, of which no account can be given other than that "God has given the condition"; the inexplicability of its occurrence in this individual rather than in this other corresponding to the mystery of election, perhaps. So narrow is the historical point upon which faith is reared that "the disciple, if he understood himself, must wish that the immediate contemporaneity should cease, by God's leaving the earth."[23] This is Kierkegaard's version of: "It is expedient for you that I go away."[24] But the same writer could declare (assuming the Johannine authorship of the Epistle): "That which we have seen and heard declare we unto you, that ye also might have fellowship with us."[25] The logic of Kierkegaard's dialectic of faith requires only tangential contacts of eternity with time, both in the incarnation and in the recurrence of faith down through the centuries. History, as such, is in the end irrelevant: faith is an event outside time.

[23] op. cit., p. 88.
[24] John 16.7.
[25] I John 1.3.

The "eternal event" of God's entrance into history is, of course, explicitly labelled paradoxical: it is "the paradox." "How does the learner come to realize an understanding with this paradox? We do not ask that he understand the paradox, but only that this is the paradox . . . It comes to pass when the reason and the paradox encounter one another happily in the "moment": when the reason sets itself aside and the paradox bestows itself. The third entity in which this union is realized (for it is not realized in the Reason, since it is set aside: nor in the Paradox, which bestows itself—hence it is realized *in* something) is that happy passion . . . *Faith*. This, then, must be the condition . . . which the Paradox contributes . . . if the Paradox does not grant this condition the learner must be in possession of it. But if the learner is in possession of the condition he is *eo ipso* himself the truth, and the "moment" is merely the moment of occasion."[26] Are we then to say that we can never hope to understand the relation of faith to the historical, because the whole transaction is outside history and understanding? Is faith a *tertium quid*, neither time nor eternity, neither history nor yet mystical elevation above history? Does the "setting aside" of reason imply irrationality or a higher rationality? That the Christian tradition has usually opted for the latter is, of course, no argument against Kierkegaard's superior insight into the relations of reason and revelation. But doubts suggest themselves from two sides.

Firstly: it is not evident beyond a doubt that Kierkegaard's version of the origin of Christian faith does not involve confidence in a degree of historical evidence in the plain sense of the term. As regards the contemporary disciple it would appear that Jesus must have made explicit His claim to be God. Now this aspect of "the fact of Christ" is not "eternal fact" but historical fact, to be proved or disproved by such processes of investigation as are open to New Testament criticism as a branch of historical studies. It may well be that such proof or disproof is not now possible. Such a claim is explicit in the pages of the Fourth Gospel, the historical value of which is in dispute among scholars. Again, we noted in passing Kierkegaard's reference to the Virgin

[26] *op. cit.*, p. 47.

Birth of Jesus, which he appeared to hold as *de fide*, and the primary historical evidence for which rested, according to him, necessarily upon the testimony of one woman. As regards the disciple at second-hand, Kierkegaard says the "occasion" for his belief is the testimony of the contemporary generation, "we have believed that in such and such a year God appeared among us" and so on. Not the "facts in the Jesus-event" here, but the *belief* that such were the "facts" in the case of those who *believed* in Jesus, where *belief* is more than a matter of assent to historical evidence. But such *belief* is—or was—itself an historical fact, the most certain fact in the whole range of Christian origins; witness the emphasis on this fact in *Formgeschichte* in our own day. The belief of the first generation of disciples is plain historical fact, transmitted by written and institutional evidence, by the sense of Scripture and the persistence of the Church. What are we to do, what have we to do, with the historical knowledge that there were men and women who so believed? Some have dismissed their belief as fanaticism or hallucination. What would happen if it were conclusively proved (for even approximation-knowledge admits on occasion of conclusive proof or disproof) that Jesus never existed? I cannot think that Kierkegaard would have pushed his view of the nature of Christian faith to this "limiting possibility" in the fashion of Paul Tillich in the first series of Aberdeen Gifford Lectures, according to the Press summary of these, and his own statement in an earlier work *The Interpretation of History*, 1936.[27] The phrase "eternal fact" seems to me to imply that this "fact" is taken for true historical occurrence. But what are later generations to make of this belief of the contemporary generation of Christian disciples? Must not faith take some stock of historical probabilities here, regarding both Jesus and the kind of people who believed in Him, all as set forth in documents whose value as mere history must be investigated? True, faith does not, cannot, wait upon the indisputable conclusion of an historical inquiry conducted by experts in such examination. But there *are* historical issues here, and the paradox of Christian faith can hardly mean taking historical decisions in the absence of, or even against,

[27] *op. cit.*, p. 33f.

the purely historical evidence. The belief of the contemporary disciple *is* enough to evoke faith on the part of a later disciple. The "Christ-idea" *can* call forth faith, and might continue to do so in face of the proof that Jesus never existed. But would this faith be the same as the faith that Very God became Very Man in the year One (or 4 B. C.) of our era in Jesus of Nazareth born of the woman Mary, who also was crucified for us under Pontius Pilate? Would the resultant faith continue to survive alongside the historical certainty that originally it arose by a mistake on certain historical matters? Would not this be to range Christian faith with lower rather than with larger sources of spiritual conviction? Is it not the negation of the classical view of the relations of Christian faith to history?

Secondly: there would be general agreement with Kierkegaard that Christian faith is not assent to historical verities as such. It is not even assent to the occurrence of an "eternal fact" as a matter of history. It is not merely acquaintance with the historical facts of Jesus' life and mission, but the perception of these as the saving acts of God in history, and the appropriation of this salvation in individual subjectivity. There is a "leap" in faith. The contemporary witness had the historical facts before him: only some took the leap of faith. The later generations of the faithful have the historical facts at second-hand, plus the assurance that some of the first generation did find in these God's presence among men. The assurance of the contemporary disciple was not arrived at by any immanental logic of conviction, says Kierkegaard. The later generations are not encouraged to believe by the example or the contagion of the faith of the first. That, too, would be immanence, the Socratic relationship which alone is possible between man and man. Any direct communication in matters of faith denies its essential quality and ethos of subjectivity. It is possible to be immensely impressed by the service Kierkegaard has rendered to the Christian religion by his stress on subjectivity, his differentiation of faith from intellectual conviction upon historical realities, his insistence on indirect communication as alone in place in this sphere of saving belief, and yet to wonder whether he has not been misled by the conception of the incarnation as "eternal fact."

Eternity and time are set over against each other as disparate incommensurables—to hold anything else is to subscribe to the Greek, the Socratic, conception of eternity as abstract timelessness. Hence the eternal fact of God's entering time at a particular point in history as an individual particular man is sheer paradox. But is the paradox, on the showing of Christian faith itself, of this metaphysical or ontological nature? Is it not rather the paradox of love stooping to lowliness and rejection, which is unbelievable apart from its happening? Is the leap of faith which sees God in Jesus Christ, meek and lowly in mind, among men in the form of a servant, submitting unto the obedience of death in the pursuit of man's love, is not this a leap akin to what Kierkegaard himself calls "the transition from a quantitative to a qualitative dialectic"? Is it not an Aristotelian *metabasis eis allo genos*, certainly of a unique and incomparable grandeur and significance, but not necessarily cutting all ties with immanence? Does the assertion of the miracle of the divine condescension in Jesus Christ deny the presence of God with His people all along in "salvation-history"? Kierkegaard's favourite Gospel combines emphasis upon the wonder of the becoming flesh of the divine Word with the doctrine that this same Word was all along in the world, the light of the life of men, by whom the worlds were made. This Word came unto His own, who should have known Him. Faith in Him, so far from being a leap into the metaphysical void, is something to be horrified at in its absence: His own received Him not. He had been present from the first, His coming had been prepared for, and should not have been met with incredulity and hostility. Is this the absolute paradox which sets at naught all that has happened and been thought elsewhere and before? The New Testament uniformly speaks of the revelation of grace and truth in Jesus Christ in the light of what was done through Moses and the prophets: it is fulfilment, not negation. Are there, then, no analogies on the "human" level, within immanence, to what happens in faith? There is a leap in the transition from fact to value, the operation of a qualitative dialectic in place of a quantitative, with its own mysteries, its own appeals to subjectivity; within whose choices we can yet detect a certain universality which justifies our conclusion that reason in the larger sense of the term is still at work. Are we compelled to desert all doctrine of the immanent presence of the divine reason in creation when we come to Christian faith, when we assert that in Jesus Christ we have "reason" to believe that the divine reason itself has come as love in search of us in our lostness in sin?

In this connection we may recall those statements of Kierkegaard which seem to posit an act of "faith" (even if only of a sort!) in our very knowledge of nature. The *Interlude* in the *Philosophical Fragments* introduced us to the fact that even nature has a history. The leap is there from the *what* of which our senses inform us to the *that* of its occurence which cannot be known immediately: existence refuses systematization. There is the paradox that something came into being that was not and now is not. By this statement Kierkegaard paved the way for what he wanted to say about faith as the basic form of ethical and religious subjectivity. It cannot but suggest doubts as to whether what he wants to say about Christian faith in particular really requires to be separated by a chasm from all other forms of truth whatsoever. Yet this is what the doctrine of the absolute paradox seems to say.

Of one possible misunderstanding we must definitely clear Kierkegaard: faith is not "the will to believe" in the sense in which later pragmatism made the phrase familiar. Faith, in its Christian version, is not presented by Kierkegaard as any high-minded choice of the noblest hypothesis— or even of the most strenuous hypothesis, for all his talk of the swimmer suspended over seventy fathoms of water, who must continuously exert himself to keep himself merely afloat. He does talk of faith as "the category of despair."[28] But he does not suggest that faith is a shrinking from the horrors of a godless universe and a taking refuge in deliberately willed optimism—a kind of whistling to keep one's courage up. The "highest passion of subjectivity" is called forth by an Object, by the very highest and greatest possible Object, by God Himself. Only the circumstances are such that the Object seems incredible. The paradox that the Deity,

[28] *Postscript*, p. 179n.

the Eternal, came into being at a definite moment in time as an individual man, is incredible apart from God's unique action in the incarnation which makes the paradox credible to and credited by the believer. "It is easy to see . . . since it is involved in the fact that reason is set aside, that faith is not an act of will; for all human volition has its capacity within the scope of an underlying condition. Thus if I have the courage to will the understanding, I am able to understand the Socratic principle, i.e. to understand myself; because from the Socratic point of view I have the condition, and so have the power to will this understanding."[29] But in Christian faith it is not a question of understanding myself at all, but of "realizing an understanding with the paradox"; which necessitates a condition which I do not of myself have and cannot give myself, but which God gives, or alternatively, the paradox "contributes" in the act of "bestowing itself."[30] I do not think Kierkegaard wants us to understand this in the sense that God creates favourable psychological dispositions in the human subject; although if we insist on trying to understand this mystery something like this special *ad hoc* creation is probably what we shall end up with. But for Kierkegaard there is no question of being by nature the sort of person to whom religion comes easy or makes appeal; or of having the spiritual insight to detect a divine significance in the person or life of Jesus, whether in the popular sense of being "spiritually minded" or in the specialized sense of possessing the faculty of "divination" in Rudolf Otto's exposition, sensitiveness to the numinous. The "condition" is what the paradox "gives" by the fact of its own appearing and in the process of commending itself to belief. It is a mystery of appropriation corresponding to the mystery of revelation. It may and ought to evoke the most strenuous effort as a consequence of all this; but it is not itself to be believed by an effort of will stifling the objections and hesitations of unbelief or disbelief. Where it is believed all the conditions of belief are in the paradox itself: it has made itself believed. The sons of God are not born of the will of man. Flesh and

[29] *Fragments*, p. 50.
[30] *op. cit.*, p. 46.

blood have not revealed it, but the Father which is in heaven.[31]

It is important to remember this aspect of the teaching of Kierkegaard. Here is a man whose major emphasis is on vital Christianity as appropriation, as the supreme energizing of subjectivity. One cannot be born a Christian, but only reborn a Christian. No inheritance of tradition and outlook, no incorporation in the visible Church by baptism, can take the place of conscious cleaving to an absolute paradox which sets at naught all life and thought else. There is an abiding *offence* or scandal to all ordinary ways of thought which must continually be annihilated by what we can only describe as an effort of will. Yet we are told the transition from unfaith to faith is not an act of will. It is a "suffering," a "passion," something that happens to us and in us, and constitutes an enduring "pathos" of the Christian life. It would not be fair, of course, to saddle Kierkegaard with all the burden of rendering intelligible the place of *will* in the Christian salvation. "It is God which worketh in you, both to will and to do of his good pleasure."[32] This language of faith is apt to seem in contradiction with Paul's further injunction in the same passage: "Work out your own salvation with fear and trembling." But does not the contradiction arise from conceiving God and man as two similar agents co-operating in analogous ways within the same field of reference? God's share in human action cannot be distinguished from man's either by dogmatic definition or psychological inspection. *Soli Deo gloria* is the language of faith on any account of the Christian position. All is of God, from whom, through whom, and unto whom are all things. But, looked at from the human end of the process, from below, there is much that man must do of and for himself. From the finite standpoint the absolute has got to be spoken of, allowed for, as if it were one term in the process, one factor in the situation, partner along with man in a joint enterprise; otherwise we have the elimination of man, the declaration of the unreality of the human point of view. The doctrine of the absolute paradox certainly means that two incommensurables are concerned in the

[31] John 1.12f.; Matt. 16.17.
[32] Phil. 2.13.

Christian salvation. But the emphasis on faith as *passion* joins oddly with an equal emphasis on it as *strenuousness*, if these are both meant to cover the same point in the process of salvation. We could conceive the latter as the result of the former easily enough, the Christian works as flowing from the Christian faith, with all the more ardour from the knowledge of the love which first loved us, with all the more diligence from the combined sense of gratitude and responsibility in the adoption of the sons of God. But Kierkegaard makes faith itself a work, if not in the first then in the second instance, if not in its inception at least in its continuance. Is the Sisyphean labour of annihilating offence in the end the characteristic note of Christian faith? Or is there to be detected here a note of torment—even perhaps of self-torment—due to some idiosyncrasy of Kierkegaard's spiritual constitution and history? Is it not even possible to detect some remaining tendency to an over-intellectualization of the concept of faith itself?

Chapter 4

The Subject Makes Itself

Heidegger and Existentialism

FROM A WELL-KNOWN anthology of Kierkegaard's writings I take the following comment by a contemporary German Catholic theologian: "Kierkegaard's conception of subjectivity and truth sets a totally different problem to European philosophy than is propounded by subjectivism and individualism, which lead to scepticism and agnosticism . . . The question is really whether the separation of the intellect from all else in man is not a special characteristic of European philosophy, whether it comes half so naturally to the Slavs as to us, while it seems that it is by no means natural to the oriental . . . European philosophy . . . proceeds from the world through the person, who is but an empty relative point, back to the world; it goes from the objects, things, sensations . . . passing as quickly as possible over the subject, the self, the individual, back to the objects, things, sensations . . . Kierkegaard does not follow this age-old development because he aims at something higher. He wishes to reverse the order and the procedure for both philosophy and thought. He wishes to go from the person over the things to the person, and not from the things over the person to the things . . ."[1] Is this a fair description of Kierkegaard's intention or accomplishment in the *Concluding Unscientific Postscript?* There is certainly a violent protest against a certain development of European thought as an intellectualistic deviation: the Hegelian philosophy has managed to forget the Subject and the individual in a presentation of the objectivized Subject or objective spirit—for Kierkegaard a contradiction in terms. But the remedy, according to Kierkegaard, is not in any anti-intellectualist depreciation of

[1] Theodore Haecker, *Sören Kierkegaard,* 1913 and 1922, pp. 25-27; quoted Bretall, *A Kierkegaard Anthology,* 1947, p. 192.

thought in favour of arbitrary practicalities of will: it is in a profounder dialectic of total human existence in its movement in time, the prime dimension of all concrete reality. It is doubtful if Kierkegaard wishes to present us with a *personalistic* account of natural science, for example, or even of history. His complaint against both kinds of knowledge is that they are abstract and constitute "approximation knowledge" at best. "From the things over the person to the things" seems to myself a formula Kierkegaard would have conceded as quite in place here, as securing the kind of objectivity appropriate to these disciplines, which he had no desire to displace or replace. "From the person over the things to the person": this is the characteristic Kierkegaardian emphasis. But his formula "subjectivity is truth" is no disparagement of objectivity, as we have seen, but rather the description of authentic personal life. Christian life "in the spirit" presents this subjectivity at its most intense, because the Object with which it is preoccupied is a unique Object which sets in reverse certain conditions of the acknowledgement of objectivity elsewhere: it is the paradox of the coming of the eternal and absolute truth into existence in an individual man at a particular moment in time. Kierkegaard holds out no hope of *our* attaining an intellectual schema of all existence from this supremely subjective point of view. Truth in that sense is for God only, not for any human Subject. For us it remains obstinately paradox and offence.

"From the person over the things to the person": this formula seems more appropriate to a movement of more recent times, philosophical in origin, but which has had profound repercussions in theology, even in the theology which most insists upon its own independence in matter and method. What is called Existentialism nowadays is not so much a school of thought, with an identical body of methodological presuppositions and practice, still less an identical corpus of philosophical findings, so much as a mood in which thinking is done by a group of thinkers of very different total quality or outlook. It so chances that, chiefly through a French exponent of extraordinary mental subtlety who is also a man of letters, the philosophical impetus has touched contemporary literature in the novel and the drama, and thus made a wider public conscious of the mood and intellectual fashion. In the literary reviews Existentialism means Jean Paul Sartre and his influence. A popular dictionary recently enough re-issued to include a definition of the term explains thus: "Existentialism, a term covering a number of related doctrines denying objective universal values and holding that a man must create values for himself through action and by living each moment to the full."[2] This is wide enough to cover Gabriel Marcel's Catholic Christian Existentialism, Karl Jaspers' secularized version of Christian themes with the theological issues muted, and Sartre's atheistic gospel, which has been greeted as specially timely for a generation exhausted by a second World War, as bidding men create meaning out of the nihilistic reduction of all ideologies, out of the nausea of the awareness of nothingness. There can be little doubt, however, that the central figure in the development of the purely philosophical side of the movement is the man from whom Sartre himself acknowledges to have learned most, namely, Martin Heidegger. *L'Être et le Néant* (1947) presupposes *Sein und Zeit* (1927). In any case Heidegger's is the version of Existentialism we must look at for our purpose, however briefly and inexpertly. For not only is he profoundly influenced by Kierkegaard and one of the main vehicles of Kierkegaard's influence upon the modern world, but Heidegger is one of the main points of contact of the new and the old Existentialism with theology proper. His is the influence which Karl Barth seeks to eliminate from his own theology in successive editions of the *Dogmatik* (particularly the famous first volume); and his is the concealed influence which critics of Rudolf Bultmann detect behind his attempts to combine philosophical elements with a theology of the Word. I regret that I cannot offer here the results of first-hand study of Heidegger's unfinished masterpiece. I shall depend mainly upon a recent and an older work of exposition and criticism, supplemented by reading of reviews and histories of recent thought. H. J. Blackham's *Six Existentialist Thinkers* (1952), in spite of extreme condensation of style, encourages me by its intelligibility to trust its account of

[2] *Chambers's Twentieth Century Dictionary,* New Mid-Century Version, 1952, *s.v.*

Heidegger and the other thinkers treated. The older work is John Cullberg's *Das Du und die Wirklichkeit* (Uppsala, 1933). The criticism and general suggestiveness of this work have been of the greatest value in my own case, and probably underlie the choice of the subject of this course of lectures.

The first impression, then, of Heidegger's thought is that here we do have an account of the nature of things very much from the standpoint of the person outwards and back again. The clear outlines of common-sense philosophy's view of things and persons have certainly become blurred, and the existences themselves appear to have become fluid, intermingling and interpenetrating each other's essences. It is a shock to have a hammer defined, not in terms of wood and steel, but in terms of its nature as a tool, its relation to human purposes. "Being-ready-to-hand" (*Zuhandenheit*) is Heidegger's description of "this type of existent." "The tool, related to other tools in an elaborate system of regular, serviceable, but modifiable relations, is the typical thing or object in the world . . . This is the primitive meaning of objects or things, and remains their fundamental concrete meaning . . . they are constituted by their relations to other things in the world and to an existent of the nature of *Dasein'* (i.e. to a human being, "the needle implies the thread, the garment, the sewer, the wearer."[3] True, there is another point of view. "The hammer can be regarded as a tool (*Zuhandene*) or as a given object (*Vorhandene*), as something ready-to-hand or merely as something at-hand, present . . . To say the hammer is heavy may mean that it is unwieldy or that it has a weight, can be weighed." In this latter type of existent the hammer comes within the purview of science. But it does not therefore fall out of relation to human beings and their needs. Science itself is a human *project* (*Entwurf*). a sketch of meaning introduced into one particular view of the world from the human perspective. The "rational construction of a world of objects in space and time," which is the aim of science, is "a co-ordinate perspective" with the "practical interpretation of the world," with which it does not conflict. "Science deals with objects from a limited point of view

[3] Blackham, *op. cit.*, p. 89.

determined in advance, limits its interest to certain phenomena and on that basis settles its methods and criteria. To regard the hammer as a body having weight is a restricted view for a special purpose. Science is not privileged but specialized, not *the* interpretation of the world but a selected aspect, not an experience in the use of a concrete object handled in the perspective of man's projects but a breakdown into abstractions taken out of the system of concrete relations and assimilated to another system of meanings determined by special questions raised within the perspective of the project of Nature."[4] Instead of premature rejoicings over this putting of science in its place as one human perspective amongst others—and a somewhat abstract one at that—it behoves us rather to consider what all this involves for Heidegger's view of the nature of both philosophic and scientific truth.

It is of the utmost importance to remember that in the published part of his philosophical undertaking Heidegger is setting forth the nature of specific human existence. *Dasein,* the "being-there" or existence which is his theme, is "the mode of existence of the human being."[5] Now, as the very title of his book *Sein und Zeit* indicates, Heidegger wishes to raise the question of *Sein,* of being, in general. His ultimate quest is the "meaning of being," *der Sinn von Sein.*[6] The pupil of Edmund Husserl, founder of the Phenomenological School, whose method he considers himself as continuing, Heidegger aims specifically at ontology, not just phenomenology. Instead of "bracketing" the real world and the experiencing Subject, Heidegger hopes by scrutiny of the human Subject in its ineluctable relations with the real world to find the clue to the nature of being as such—if and in so far as it may prove possible that this should be found. "The *nature* of being as such"? He himself talks rather of the "meaning of being." Ontology is after all itself a rational inquiry, an activity of the human mind. That the word "ontology" can be split into the two components of *ontos* and *logos,* being and reason (thought), does not involve an affirmative answer to the question whether we can ever attain to

[4] All quotations from Blackham, *op. cit.,* p. 90.
[5] Blackham, *op. cit.,* p. 88.
[6] Cullberg, *op. cit.,* p. 102.

an intuition of what being looks like apart from thought or experience. Phenomenology, from which Heidegger derives, is itself the heir of German idealism. "In so far as phenomenology seeks to determine the objects which it grasps, not as they are in themselves but in terms of the act of consciousness" which apprehends them "it once again approximates to Kantian lines of thought."[7] At any rate Heidegger argues that "since we are not outside being and able to stand in relation to it as we do to an object of thought, we shall have to proceed indirectly by examining particular types of existents. Human existence is obviously indicated as the starting-point, since we are privileged in our relation to that, and since any metaphysic of being must itself be a product of this human existent. The first task is to uncover the structure of this human existence."[8] In any case "human existence is the only point where the ontic and the logical intersect":[9] where else could *ontology* begin? The result will be a *meaning*, the meaning of being. It need not therefore be an "existentialist" reading of the meaning of being, for all that it sets out from the *Existenz* of the human subject, from *Dasein*. "Heidegger insistently dissociates himself from existential philosophy, for, he says, he is concerned with the problem of being, not with personal existence and its ethical interests, the human condition as such."[10] It is important to remember this. Heidegger is aiming at the phenomenological "intuition of being" (*phänomenologisches Wesenschau*), and where he uses language which involves human concern with environment, both human and inanimate, where he might appear to be evaluating things in terms of persons—as in his talk of *Sorge* or *concern* as central to his view of the world—he still aims at objective description of the most general order, untouched by any ethical implication. This is a matter to which we shall return. Meanwhile we reiterate that, for all his seeming involvement of things with persons, their purposes and perspectives and projects, Heidegger conceives himself as carrying on a rigidly *objective* tradition in philoso-

[7] Ernst von Aster, *Geschichte der Philosophie*, 1950, p. 394.
[8] Blackham, *op. cit.*, p. 88.
[9] Cullberg, *op. cit.*, p. 102.
[10] Blackham, *op. cit.*, p. 86.

phy. Only, philosophy can and must yield a *meaning*, even where it talks about being. Like science, it too is a *project*, a perspective, an ideal construction of existence, that "inexhaustible reservoir of meanings."[11] Thought is thought: the shadow of the thinker falls over his landscape. Man cannot step out of his shadow or his skin when he talks about being. That does not mean that relation to human thought or to human concerns is a feature of the final nature of being. Indeed, Heidegger appears to believe that the ultimate nature of things is indifferent to such concerns. Man and all his works go out in the end into nothingness.

With these warnings in view we look very briefly at the main points in Heidegger's account of *Dasein*, of the characteristic nature of human being. In the first place, a new moral is drawn from an old truth. It cannot be said that idealism had ever really forgotten the fact that the nature of the knowing Subject is consciousness, and, more specifically still, self-consciousness. But at last there is a real attempt to give effect to the Hegelian position that Subject does not mean substance. Even when it meant better, idealism had tended to think of the Subject as a thing amongst things, however; made of a different material, perhaps; but still a monad of spiritual "stuff." Though not lending itself to such pictorial imagination, Hegelianism had yet contrived to forget the Subject amid its objective manifestations, in knowledge, art, religion and political life. Now there is a new insistence that "the essence of *Dasein* is in its existence."[12] The title of Heidegger's book reminds us that *time* rather than *space* is the dimension of the human Subject's reality. "Man is a being with no substance but with a history." This declaration of a famous theologian of our time, when he comes to the anthropological division of his dogmatics, betrays an awareness begotten of the work of Heidegger in contemporary philosophy, and is one more indication of the interdependence of theology and philosophy, whatever the purist theories and intentions of the former discipline. It would be too soon, however, to conclude that the category of substance has been altogether banished from philosophico-theological thinking,

[11] Blackham, *op. cit.,* p. 88.
[12] *ibid.*

either in the concept of things or persons. One may have doubts whether *Existenz*, actuality in temporal succession, is ready and able to take over all the functions formerly ascribed to substance. But however that may be, it cannot be denied that the analysis of Subject in the new style of thought has been immensely significant and suggestive. Human existence is not only that which exists but which is *conscious* of itself as existence, as existing. Once again, this had always been known. But in the new context of *Existenz* versus substance it means that the human Subject does not fall all on the one side of the fence between (epistemological) Subject and Object: in its most characteristic operation the Subject is its own Object. A Subject is that which exists for itself as possibility, as infinite possibilities, as a realized selection from particular possibilities in the past, and a realizable selection of particular possibilities in the future. As a later existentialist writer puts it: a human being is *un être qui se fait*—a being that makes itself (Louis Lavelle). "The self is not a reality which is given but a reality which seeks itself."[13] All this was there for finding in Kierkegaard, of course; but it needed the Kierkegaard renaissance to make it available, and Heidegger's is the first master-construction in the new style. Transcendence is of the very essence of the Subject or self. Indeed it not so much *is* as *has been* and now *is not,* and *will be* what it now *is not.* It is somehow a possibility poised between two nothingnesses. Instead of being a closed circle round a central point, it is a room with the windows and doors open to all winds and sunshine it can catch—perhaps, in view of the characteristic existentialist picture of the human situation or predicament, one should say rather, open to all the storms that blow.

This "openness" of the self receives further qualification by Heidegger in the doctrine that *Dasein,* fundamental human existence, is "being-in-the-world," *In-der-Welt-Sein.* Not merely does the self happen to be one thing in a universe of other things (indeed, of course, it is not a *thing* at all), but its very *Existenz* is constituted by its relations to its environment, the *Umwelt* of things and other persons. Things, we

[13] Louis Lavelle; quoted V. Gollancz, *A Year of Grace,* 1950, p. 411.

have seen, are essentially its *tools*. This is not just a statement in technology. Digressing for a moment from the question of how tools may make the man, how the machine may turn master of the man, how a man's occupation and recreation may constitute him the kind of person he is; we repeat that Heidegger's position as regards the tool quality of "things" is not a reversion to the anthropomorphic teleology of eighteenth-century Christian apologetics, for which the moon was a lantern hung in the sky to light human travellers by night. "The abstract geometric space of mathematical physics contrasts with the qualitative space of actual preoccupations, which is inseparable from the objects: the place where the object is determines its nature and conditions its function; the brake is not a brake unless it is on the wheel, and its being in place in turn creates the stable conditions of the environment."[14] If the "qualitative space of actual preoccupations . . . is inseparable from the objects," then this is a two-way truth: not only are "things" *tools* in their very essence or existence, but man, the tool-maker and tool-user—*homo faber*— must also be conceived as living in that same "qualitative space" with his tools, making and being made by them. As for persons, the self is constituted equally in its very thoughts, feelings, actions, by its relations to other selves as by its commerce with things. Heidegger's statements here work upon us with less effect of novelty than in his account of things, because the ground had already been partly covered by earlier idealism. Only he gives the feeling of taking the mutual interpenetration and implication of selves more literally and seriously, because the monadistic self-containedness of spiritual substance appears to have been more completely given up. Moreover, the older idealism was usually concerned to exhibit this mutual implication of selves in the interests of such universal spiritual values as science, morality, citizenship, religion. Heidegger gives it a more "objective," matter-of-fact cast in accordance with his phenomenological preoccupation, by coming back to persons through things. "My being-in-the-world, in this sense of being constituted by my projects and by my relations with the objects which I make use of and develop as tools for realizing

[14] Blackham, *op. cit.*, p. 89.

them, involves my being-with-others who are also in the world in the same sense. Here again the existence of others is not merely accidental, nor a problem for thought, but it is a necessity of thought, is constitutive of my being and implied in it, as the barber implies the customer, and the needle as needle both the thread and the cloth, and the seamstress the wearer. The nature of *Dasein* is being-in-common, human existence is a shared existence and the social interdependence of our everyday experience is primordial and constitutive. My full self-consciousness and self-affirmation derive from my consciousness of others; it is not that I begin with myself as given and indubitable and somehow deduce the existence of others like myself. Thus I am constituted both by my preoccupations in which I make use of objects as tools and by my solicitude for persons."[15] On both sides of this relatedness human existence is summed up as *Mit-Sein,* "being-with" both things and persons, because these are the two fundamental aspects of "begin-in-the-world." And the other self is fundamentally my *Mit-Mensch,* my fellow-man, the man I am "along with" in the world, essentially and not accidentally. Togetherness is of the nature of things, constitutive of essence as existence.

This relatedness, this essential preoccupation of the human Subject with his environment of things and persons, in his thought-life, his work and play, his politics and his poetry, in all the aspects of his day-to-day life, exterior and interior, is summed up by Heidegger in his doctrine that "the innermost essence of human existence (the '*being* in human-*being*') is *Sorge.*"[16] This central term in the Heideggerian vocabulary almost defeats translation: "care" is the most neutral rendering; "concern would often be more appropriate because more colourless. But already Heidegger wishes to exploit this equivocality. *Sorge* cannot help being coloured in all German uses by the darker emotional associations of its primary meaning. "Uneasiness, anxiety, trouble . . . grief, sorrow"; so runs the list of dictionary synonyms.[17] Heidegger's choice of this term for the fundamental feature of

[15] Blackham, *op. cit.,* p. 90f.
[16] Cullberg, *op. cit.,* p. 102.
[17] *Cassell's German Dictionary,* 1936, *s.v.*

human existence soon shows itself to be in no way uncon-
sidered or unaware of the emotional overtones. Certainly it
allows him to choose two further compounds of the root
word (after the convenient fashion of the German language,
which almost persuades us that this is the native speech of
philosophical discussion) to indicate the differentiation which
Sorge undergoes according as it is directed towards or im-
plicated in things and persons respectively. Concern for or
with the *Umwelt* of things is named *Besorgen*, while *Füsorge*
expresses the implication of *Dasein* in the *Mitwelt* of persons.
These terms might conceivably be divested of feeling, but
scarcely so the quartet of *Angst, Tod, Gewissen, Schuld*—
anxiety, death, conscience and guilt. These explicate the
conception of *Sorge* as the human condition in its *Verfallensein*, its state of fall and deliverance to destruction, in this
temporal existence. If Kant astonished his rationalist contemporaries of the Enlightenment with a philosophical doctrine of Original Sin, he was at least going against the pre-
vailing mood of his century, which optimistically looked to
reason to banish the shadows of ignorance and superstition
from a baleful tyranny of centuries over the human race. Has
Heidegger then merely succumbed to the disillusionment and
pessimism which have become the emotional ground-tone
of the first half of the twentieth century in his doctrine of
Sorge, Angst and *Verfallensein*?

For his own part Heidegger professes merely to be speaking
according to the nature of reality as it discloses itself to
Wesenschau, the consistent and impartial scrutiny of being,
which is the methodological principle of phenomenology.
There are two results or findings of such plain looking at
human existence which impel us to a sombre, not to say
tragic, summing up of the situation; and both in their
manner proceed from the evisceration of the substantial self.
In the first place, the opening of the confines of the self to
a fluid commingling or interpenetration of selves, my being
made up, as it were, of my relations to other existents, means
that in a great many departments of my day-to-day existence
I live at an almost impersonal level of personal life. In the
vast majority of human relationships men are not authentic
selves or individuals. They are the reflection of unreflective

attitudes, the subjective facets of mass opinion and emotions. The true Subject of action, feeling and thought in these is "man" in general, *Das Man*. This impersonal one is "the ubiquitous dictator of human affairs."[18] To belong to "the public" is to be subjected to a process "by which each one in a necessary conformity to established usages, judgements and opinions is assimilated to the general forms of human existence."[19] Consciously to rebel against this process is not therefore to escape its influence; it may merely land the rebel in the cult of eccentricity or nonconformity. In any case it is easier to swim with the tide; the forces of inertia and the pleasures of conformity are too much for most men. The situation may be more common in our century and exaggerated by the political and technological trends of the times. But it is not peculiar to our age; it is a permanent feature of the human situation and condition, depending on human nature as a "being-with-others" or *Mit-Sein*. This is the substance of "day-to-day life," which as *Alltäglichkeit* is yet another technical term in the Heideggerian vocabulary. But this unfortunate state of affairs is a small matter compared with a more devastating aspect of *Dasein*. Not only is the nature of the self as transcendence nothing substantial, a "possibility poised between two nothingnesses," as we have described it. As temporal existence (*zeitliche Existenz*) it is bracketed between two actual, factual nothingnesses, my non-existence before birth and the termination of my existence by death, which negates all further possibilities in the future when it does occur, and by anticipation devalues all possibilities, including realized possibilities, in the present. The fundamental truth about life is that it must die. It came out of nothing and will shortly return into nothing. The back drop against which the tragicomedy of human existence is played is a blank. The final dimension of the human predicament is—Nothing; which the comicality of human pretension insists upon spelling with a capital "N"!

It is at this point, of course, that Existentialism impinges upon literature. The contemporary novel and drama, especially where they come under the influence of Hei-

[18] Blackham, *op. cit.*, p. 91.
[19] *ibid.*

degger's greatest disciple, Jean Paul Sartre, and his school, ring the changes upon the modern realization of the insubstantiality of the self and the meaninglessness of human life, the nausea of nothingness which besets man as he looks over the parapet walls of his day-to-day avocations and routine reactions. The absolute devaluation of all absolutes is the only absolute left to us! In its full strength this awareness is in the awakened only, although gradually it is filtering through to the vast majority, whose behaviour makes up the life of impersonal humanity, *Das Man*. "Sirs, what must we do then to be saved"? The answer is certainly that it is high time to awake out of sleep—but not that Christ or any other may give us light! For the message is not that we are passed from death unto life. Rather, we must live with our eyes filled with the certainty and sovereignty of death. Then at least we shall be filled out with the only kind of substantiality that remains to us. In the death of all meaning, all validity other than fleeting and temporal: with God Himself dead, as Nietzsche long ago told us, and the last vestiges of metaphysical magic eliminated from His substitutes—objective morality or spirituality: in this vacuum we may yet *choose* to create our own absolutes, temporary and provisional as they must be, conditional and determined by the set-up of our circumstances, personal and social. ("I am sad, French, and a waiter," to use M Sartre's example. Yet because I know these things about myself, I am to that extent distinct from them, even *free* to adjust my life in terms of them.) Then at least we shall be living authentic human existence, as individuals, not as components of *Das Man*. Then we shall have accepted our original and final nothingness and have made something of it. But we must awake and choose: awake to the anguish (*Angst*) of being found in a world to which we are bound, and which reveals its own and our emptiness. But though we are "the hollow men," all need not "end with a whimper." We can look death in the face, imitate our medieval forebears who kept a human skull on their study-tables to prop up their books, and arrange life in terms of death. Oddest of all the consequences of insubstantiality is enfranchisement: we are free—or may become so. Choice, not chance, is king in this world of shadows. We make (or we do not make) ourselves in the interval before we are again unmade, this time for good.

Once again we must remind ourselves that in all this Heidegger does not conceive himself to be speaking the language of poetry, oratory, rhetoric, or indeed any speech touched with feeling. He is talking the prose of phenomenological analysis. He is not even trenching upon the evaluations of the ethical. He is describing the structure of human being, distinguishing between authentic and inauthentic forms of *Dasein*. He is a philosopher, not a pulpiteer. He gives an account of conscience (*Gewissen*) and reinstates the idea of guilt (or owedness, *Schuld*) in the concern (*Sorge*) which has been awakened by anguish (*Angst*) to the fallen state (*Verfallenheit*) of day-to-day existence (*Alltäglichkeit*). He does not present humanity with any categorical imperative to advance to the resolvedness (*Entschlossenheit*) which distinguishes authentic from unauthentic human existence (*eigentliches versus uneigentliches Dasein*). In real history (*Geschichtlichkeit*) authentic human existence realizes that true temporality which is the meaning of human existence (*Zeitlichkeit als Sinn des Daseins*). There is, presumably, no point in asking *why* we should be authentic human beings. "A question not to be asked." There is an approximation here to Kierkegaard's conception of faith as the supreme exercise of subjectivity. Just as the Subject's keeping in constant view the absolute paradox is its maximum self-assertion, so resolvedness, choice of meaning in face of the absolute reduction of all meaning in face of death, gives to *Entschlossenheit* the greatest possible amount of *Sein* in *Dasein*, of being in human being. And so Phenomenology issues in Existentialism, despite protests to the contrary. But is this conclusion of Heidegger's a datum of pure phenomenology? Does the exposition keep itself at the level of the completely unethical scrutiny of factual existence? Is this the one and only possible reading of the nature of human existence from the "facts," objective, necessary, from the nature of the case? Or is it only one version of the situation amongst several possibles? He is probably right in refusing the suggestion that the choice in face of death should be

its anticipation in suicide. After all, it is the nature of existence we are discussing, not that of non-existence, of life,
not death—even although the cardinal truth about life is that
it must die. Life itself must go on, if only in order to have
no ultimate meaning! But is his conclusion of the *meditatio
mortis* the only possible one? "Let us eat, drink and be merry,
for tomorrow we die." What is wrong with the Epicurean
conclusion, purely on the phenomenological level? Again, if
choice and resolvedness be the test of authentic human
existence, why should "Evil, be thou my good!" be ruled out.
The devil is represented in Christian tradition as a very
resolved and highly integrated personality. It is often said
that Satan is the real hero of the Miltonic epic, which sets
out to "justify the ways of God to men." "Heidegger points
out a philosophy cannot pretend to prescribe to the individual
what he shall do (least of all an existential philosophy,
which insists on the uniqueness of the concrete individual).
It gives the general determination of human being, the
master perspective which commands all possibilities: the
concrete decisions, the actual possibilities of each personal
existence to be realized in daily life, are left to the make-up
and history of the person and to his liberty and the circumstances of the case."[20] Very good: many Christian moralists
can be found similarly expounding the liberty of the children
of God. Heidegger clearly conceives that not only should human life go on, but that men should choose good rather than
evil, that the broadly accepted cultural tasks of civilization
will prescribe in outline what can only be called an ethics.
But how does it come about that the authentic form of human
existence should thus coincide generally with the pursuit of
good? Even if this be granted as a phenomenological finding,
is it not a momentous one? If there is this interpenetration
of fact and value, should not this finding be given greater
scope in any reading of the final nature of reality? If the
ontic is susceptible of logical arrangement in the thought-
projects of the human being, what is ontology to make of this
further discovery that there is a factual grounding of value in
existence? Nay! has the distinction of "authentic versus inauthentic human existence" not already betrayed the in-

[20] Blackham, *op. cit.*, p. 98.

escapable presence in reason, in *logos* dealing with *ontos*, of an ethical element? The status of this element, its origin and its validity in the formation of thought-projects of reality are problems still left on our hands, when such an analysis as Heidegger's is completed. The alternative, for instance, of a "humanist" as opposed to a "religious" reading of human existence, still remains for whatever kind of argumentation is relevant.

Some little while back it was suggested that a great deal of Heidegger might have been collected from characteristic positions of Kierkegaard. There is a coincidence in the matter of the importance of *choice* in the making of the self or Subject: this is indeed one possible interpretation of the doctrine that "subjectivity is truth." The "insubstantiality" of the self, too, is anticipated in Kierkegaard's emphasis on becoming, and the *Existenz* of the Subject as temporal becoming. The existentialist mythology of Nothing could even be derived from certain expressions of Kierkegaard about the transition from non-existence to existence by the non-rational fact of "happening." But there is one thing at least to which there is no counterpart in Kierkegaard which, perhaps implicit only in Heidegger, is explicit in some of his modern existentialist followers. Kierkegaard contemplates the acquiring of such substantiality as the Subject is capable of by its appropriation of an Object, of a truth which is valid independently of such appropriation. In other words, the Kierkegaardian Subject may conceivably "make itself," but it does not "create values," give objectivity where none exists apart from its act. The Christian life is the filling of the human being with a divine content, as faith appropriates the paradox. Although this last is adhered to as "an objective uncertainty," this refers to the organ and method of appropriation of a unique Object—but still, of an *Object*. The Christian values deriving therefrom may only be recognized as such by faith. But Kierkegaard holds—quite obviously—that God and His revelation in Christ are "there," objective, even metaphysical realities, which "should," "ought," to be recognized, which assert a claim to recognition theoretically capable of coming home to all men's business and bosoms.

It may be doubted whether the last remnants of such an

"objective" conception of the character of ethical and spiritual values has entirely disappeared from Heidegger's standpoint, as a vestigial survival from the German idealism of which phenomenology is the descendent. We have just mentioned statements of his which appear to imply a universal validity —even if only a "humanist" validity—of agreed cultural tasks. But his nihilism and denial of theism take away the metaphysical background against which an objective reading of values has usually been held. If there is any room left for a quasi-objectivity of spiritual values it can only be an objectivity which human existence creates or confers. Any universality of agreement on what constitutes specific values can only derive from certain standard or uniform structures or patterns of human existence and living. It can only be understood in the context of autonomy, whereas Kierkegaard's values are theonomous. Man makes himself, for Kierkegaard, by conforming to, by taking to himself the gift of God which issues in a way of life. In Existentialism proper man makes himself in the sense of "creating value." It is, of course, possible to doubt whether this conception is not in the end self-contradictory!

It would seem that in some forms of Existentialism the creation of value goes beyond what Heidegger himself would allow. Autonomy is pressed to its utmost exercise in the choice of purely personal, even anti-social values and conduct. There is an approximation to the satanic "Evil, be thou my good!" in a way that goes beyond Heidegger's attempt to provide an ethic for nihilism. Consider this from a review of a recent book on the notorious Marquis de Sade by Simone de Beauvoir: "For Mlle de Beauvoir, the chief interest of Sade lies not in his sexual aberrations but 'in the manner in which he assumed responsibility for them.' In other words we are presented with Sade as an existentialist hero."[21] Existentialism, in its French literary development, can thus be identified with a solipsistic autonomy which justifies itself by "accepting responsibility" for anti-social conduct. This is surely the end of all "objectivity" in the sphere of value! Anything and everything is lawful, provided I accept responsibility for my own choice. But why talk about

[21] *Times Literary Supplement*, August 28, 1953, p. 543.

"responsibility" at all? Has not objective ethics returned with this word through the back door after being cast out at the front? "Value" is a kind of reason; and we must either allow it some say in the view we construct of the world—which means we must give up our nihilism, whether for humanism or a religious world-view—or we must cast out the offending word with Logical Positivism (apparently *logical* here!) as a mere interjection of feeling or exclamation mark. Heidegger himself appears to be evidence of an ambiguity on this point, which must be cleared up. Existentialism can only be or provide a way of living for these disillusioned times in the wreckage and chaos of post-war Europe (as such it has been hailed in certain quarters), not simply if men agree to accept certain values, take responsibility for their choice, and live up to their requirements, in the face of the apparent death of all meaning in the universe and the collapse of all the ideologies, but *if* it also happens that the values so accepted are constructive and not destructive—which at once raises ethical and metaphysical problems afresh! Self-choice, responsibility for choice, the willing and positing of value where the universe seems to cry out upon the existence of objective norms, and man is left naked and alone with his power of choosing—in such a situation *what* shall we choose? Subjectivity will not save us! The Object returns, inevitably. Extreme Existentialism has forgotten that a Subject without an Object is nothing at all. This abstraction cannot choose anything!

It is inevitable that Christian theologians should have been interested in Martin Heidegger. For the gospel itself is "good news" in face of a realization that man is under sentence of death, that human existence is *Sein zum Tode*, both in its physical and in its moral aspects; and the gospel calls for a total transvaluation of all values in the light of this fact—and of God's dealing with our human situation in Jesus Christ. The "good news" *is* that God *is* dealing with this situation; and this assurance belongs, of course, not to the generalities discoverable by phenomenological analysis of the human situation, but to faith which finds God so dealing in Jesus Christ. The theologian who stands nearest to Heidegger and borrows most assistance in his exposition of the Christian standpoint from Heidegger is Rudolf Bultmann. Bultmann's special position is that theology differs from philosophy by occupying itself with *believing* human existence. He shares Heidegger's methodological presuppositions, believing that a pre-theological philosophical ontology must "seek for the concepts which will express the being of human existence as far as may be with neutral concern for the nature of the object or thing itself."[22] Believing human existence, then, sees death, not just as the term of human existence in general and the devaluation of all his endeavour as vanity of vanities, but as the revelation of the judgement and grace of God, calling for decision for or against love. "Decision" (*Entscheidung*) not "resolvedness" (*Entschlossenheit*) as in Heidegger; and choice of love in particular. There is a twofold advance upon Heidegger in Bultmann. First, the point is made that Heidegger's analysis of human existence being formal and general cannot object to the particularization which it receives at the hands of theology in treating of *believing* human existence. Phenomenology is ontology; theology adds an onto-factual determination of historical human existence.[23] Second, taking a cue from the theology of Gogarten, Bultmann asserts that "real or genuine history" (*echte Geschichte*) is present only where love acknowledges the claim made upon human existence by the "Thou." However high-minded, serious and impressive the total appeal of Bultmann's existential reading of the Christian message— and it seems to be all these—it is surely impossible not to feel that by entering upon the sphere of "believing human existence" another dimension has been added to phenomenological analysis which stretches the method to breaking-point. Is phenomenology the proper context in which to assess the ultimate significance (if one hesitates over the word "metaphysical") of such concepts as "love," the "Thou" (with its ethical implication), and "genuine history"? Are these determinable at the onto-factual level—or, is what is so determinable about them the significant or characteristic thing about them? To call the Heideggerian *Mitmensch* a "Thou" is to step over the fence so carefully erected to keep

22 Cullberg, *op. cit.*, p. 106.
23 Cullberg, *op. cit.*, p. 107.

apart the ethical and the phenomenological. "Genuine versus ungenuine history" is a contrast comparable with Heidegger's "authentic versus unauthentic history"; and it is hard to see where this principle of evaluation has come from, if not from the ethical realm. And the final question is whether *value* does not cease to be value when it is treated as phenomenological ontology. If we say we are aware of all this, and are now consciously in the sphere of theology, it remains to inquire whether the phenomenological prolegomena are either necessary or even helpful. The relevance of the existential contribution is a different matter, which must be examined on its own merits.

Is Heidegger's analysis as presuppositionless as it pretends? The preliminary elimination of the ethical is surely a major presupposition! Can the being in human being be neutrally and objectively discriminated if this element is declared in advance to be no fundamental constituent of its very *Existenz?* Is it not in some sort a relic of the old "metaphysical" approach in terms of substance to regard this relationship as accidental and not inherent—that so-called "facts" are fundamental, values something superadded? The doubt remains even although this terminology be rejected.

Finally, consider this from Mr. Blackham's valuable exposition of Heidegger: "In the act of transcendence, by which personal existence separates itself from what-is and even from its own brute existence and its solidified past, its freedom and its affirmative and originative force lie in its nothingness, and it is then close to being. This separation from brute existence and from the intelligible world and from one's own past, followed by the willed identification with one's situation and assumption of one's past and fate, followed by realization of one's possibilities in the world, and again by a separation from this which devalues it and counts it as nothing, this is a mode of conjugation of Subject and Object expressing a total response of man in a total alertness and openness of being."[24] It is impressive in so brief a context to meet with two references to "brute existence." Here is a reminder that *Sein und Zeit* purports to be only the preliminary half of an undertaking: the mean-

[24] Blackham, *op. cit.,* p. 105.

ing of being is to be approached through an analysis of human being, declared the only possible approach for ontology. It is worth pointing out that no conceivable "conjugation of Subject and Object" can dispense finally with the conception of "brute existence." Existence, "that inexhaustible reservoir of meanings,"[25] is in the end merely and absolutely given; yet it is more than any or the sum of all meanings which in science, technology and the concerns of everyday life the Subject elaborates on this given basis, a basis which is *not* a meaning, nor a thought, but just *is,* is being. It may be an impossible task to think away thought from being: thought and being may belong together in a way that passes thought to isolate and express. But things are what they are, whatever the implication of some or all of them in thought, and we may even in thought have some inferred idea or conjecture of the nature of "things-in-themselves"; we may even have some experience of this. Personal existence, so completely eviscerated of substance by Heidegger, so resolved without residue into nothing as "self-transcendence," has yet its own aspect of brute existence. The self must needs be something, in order even to transcend itself; and psychology, the scientific study of the self and its behaviour, is not an irrelevance. "Things," too, have their own, if a different kind of mere being, of brute existence. The hammer *is* wood and steel and not just a tool in the carpenter's hand. The Subject of personal existence is not just thought, ideality, consciousness, self-consciousness, which are the aspects emphasized in any account of it as transcendence. It is furthermore embodied spirit, a kind of being that unites the peculiar kinds of being of both thought and things. We have our own peculiar experience, not just of nothing, which Heidegger has so eloquently expounded, but of being what we are. This might conceivably qualify for the name of Existentialism. But it is doubtful whether Existentialism, from Heidegger, who disclaims the label, to Sartre, who has made it the present vogue in literary and "intellectual" circles, would be content with the modest conclusion that the approach to the mystery of things "out over persons to things and back to persons" has not so much illumined the mystery of total

[25] Blackham, *op. cit.,* p. 88.

reality, as thrown some light—brilliant, if disillusioning—on some departmental problems of human life set against a background of limitation, fate, and—if to use the term be not to take ourselves too seriously—tragedy.

Chapter 5

Subject-Object And I-Thou

Martin Buber

THE ONTOLOGY WHICH would hold the ethical at arm's length in determining the nature of the being in which man shares, which describes his human environment as *Mitwelt* and his fellow-man as *Mitmensch*, would seem to be left far behind in a view which makes fundamental a distinction between two primary words, *I-It* and *I-Thou*. More indeed than an ethical reference is involved in the terminology in which Martin Buber offers his analysis of the human situation. But that this analysis itself marks a distinctive contribution to our understanding of the matter "What is man"? is witnessed to by the extraordinary vogue and far-reaching influence of the little book in which it is expounded. Written between autumn 1919 and spring 1922 and published in 1923, *I and Thou* has proved "one of the epoch-making books of our generation."[1] Buber's own strong religious interest has made the book of special concern to theologians. This indeed seems to have been the channel by which various existential influences have been brought to bear upon much modern theological writing, judging from the frequency with which formulas from *I and Thou* are met with there. Karl Heim uses the distinction between worlds of I-It, I-Thou, and the eternal Thou as the "dimensions" of reality which he elaborates theologically in *Glaube und Denken*.[2] The term *Gegenwart*, difficult to render adequately in English, but standing for the special living quality of the reality present in the meeting of *I* and *Thou*, has provided a theme which E. Grisebach has treated specially in the realm of ethical community. *Meeting (Begegnung)* or encounter has itself become a slogan in

[1] *I and Thou* by Martin Buber, translated by Ronald Gregor Smith, 1937, "Translator's Introduction," p. v.
[2] E. T., *God Transcendent*, 1935.

theological discussion, and this term, too, derives from Buber, who declares "All real living is meeting."[3] There are testimonies from many quarters to the radical transformation effected by *I and Thou* in a person's whole life and thinking. Thus Leslie Paul says of Buber's main thesis: "If once we grasp the tremendous import of this idea, so profound and so simple, it cannot but change our understanding and our lives."[4] Whether or not "the discovery of the Thou" (which according to Buber himself dates from Feuerbach [1804-72], but which has been brought into fertilizing contact with modern thought chiefly through his own work) deserves to be called "a Copernical revolution as rich in consequences as the idealist discovery of the I . . . pointing us beyond the Cartesian contribution to modern philosophy" may be doubtful.[5] Heim himself, the author of this statement, seems to have some hesitations about this claim; for a similar passage in earlier editions of *Glaube und Denken* was not repeated in the third. But that it could ever have been made by a theologian of his standing shows the measure of the impression made by *I and Thou*.

We begin our discussion of Buber with a quotation from one who acknowledges heavy indebtedness to "that small work . . . so radiant with the love of God and which has had so marked an influence upon our times."[6] Leslie Paul writes: "Martin Buber has most sharply distinguished between what he calls the *I-It* relation and the *I-Thou* relation . . . this distinction implies that our knowledge of nature is *of a different order* from our knowledge of persons. We know things impersonally, as objects which exist beyond us and are impenetrable by us; but we do not know other persons with whom we are intimate in this way—we meet and address them, they live in us and we in them."[7] This seems, as the writer here says, a fairly "clear intellectual distinction." But we must not take it that thereby a rigid ontological classification of the contents of the world as either "things" or "per-

[3] *op. cit.,* p. 11.

[4] *The Meaning of Human Existence,* 1949, p. 149.

[5] Karl Heim, *Zeitschrift für Theologie und Kirche,* 1930, p. 333; quoted in Buber, *Between Man and Man,* 1947, p. 148n.

[6] Leslie Paul, *op. cit.,* p. 131.

[7] *loc. cit.*

sons" is intended. Buber envisages the possibility of *I-Thou* relationships with "things": I can have an *I-Thou* relationship with a tree, for example, or with the whole created universe focused in one, in contact or meeting; and, on the other side, *I* can be related to persons impersonally. It is indeed "the exalted melancholy of our fate, that every *Thou* in our world must become an *It*."[8] It is, in the end, according to Buber's explicit wording, in the very opening sentence of *I and Thou*, a distinction in man's *attitude* to his world: "To man the world is twofold, in accordance with his twofold attitude."[9] There is some evidence that these introductory words have been forgotten, or their implications overlooked, in certain of the paeans which have celebrated the "liberation" effected by Buber in the intellectual outlook of our times. In Buber, as truly as in Heidegger, the "meaning of being" is approached by way of an analysis of human being—perhaps, of course, the only possible approach for an ontology; but one which Heidegger, at any rate, sets out by declaring as only one half of his purposed undertaking. If Buber marks an advance upon Heidegger in speaking of *Thou* at all, in giving the clear impression that man conducts a dialogue with his world and not a monologue, there is still a fundamental question left upon our hands concerning the ontological validity of the *Thou*. Is it a *real* dialogue, or one which man "conducts," there being a possible implication that the "conducting" is appearance only, from his side of the relation? The *Thou* is, of course, literally in place (although it presents its own problems of analysis) when the other term in the *I-Thou* relation is another person. It is from the peculiar mutuality of this relationship that the specific quality is taken which leads Buber to designate other relationships with impersonal or supra-personal realities which present this quality of mutuality (or appear to do so) by the extended use of the term *I-Thou* relationship. The fundamental problem of the justification of this extension, and of what modifications in our view of the ultimate nature of things it calls for and sanctions, are matters which must be postponed until we have more of Buber's schema in view.

[8] *I and Thou.*, p. 16.
[9] *op. cit.*, p. 3.

Before we look at Buber's extended use of the *Thou*, let us look briefly at what he has to say about the *I-Thou* relationship in the sphere of ethics and community life, where the *Thou* is another human person, and the term is therefore used in its basic and ordinary sense. The "discovery of the *Thou*," in the sense in which relation *with* a *Thou* is intrinsically different from relation *to* an *It* or thing, must surely, so far as modern philosophy is concerned, be credited to Kant. "Act always so as to treat humanity, whether in thine own person or in that of of another, as an end-in-itself and not as a means." This formula for the concretion of the categorical imperative already covers that meeting with the "other" in his wholeness, and not as one item in a collection or collocation of bounded units or objects; that encounter in which the "other" fills all my firmament and excludes consideration of him in relation to limited aims and projects, which Buber so eloquently expounds as the heart of the *I-Thou* relation.[10] Kant having prepared the way in this fashion, Buber's pages can be readily understood in which he describes the plight of modern man in the depersonalized world of machines and mass politics. Man degraded to a cog in a machine, to the plaything of impersonal economic laws, to a number on a card-index in a bureaucrat's office; the impoverishment of spiritual life in a technological civilization, where inventions abound and power to use profitably has decayed; where man's boasted scientific achievement looks like compassing his annihilation—all these are themes on which the prophets of our time have discoursed amply for a generation past; and for their text some at least have been under debt to Martin Buber, whether at first-hand or further remove.

It is significant that in *I and Thou* Buber does not have much to say about ethics in the strict sense. There are asides or ethical issues. There is a discourse on true love, for instance, demolishing the sentimentalists, and reducing this most personal of personal relationships to a matter of will or attitude, rather than of feeling. "Love is responsibility of an *I* for a *Thou*."[11] This sounds ethical enough. But Buber is quick

[10] See *op. cit.*, p. 8; " . . . whole in himself, he is *Thou* and fills the heavens."

[11] *op. cit.*, p. 15.

to show that ethics is not enough. No man by taking thought can add to his ethical stature one cubit, nor produce the reality of marriage by making resolutions in the void. "Marriage . . . will never be given new life except by that out of which true marriage always arises, the revealing by two people of the *Thou* to one another. Out of this a marriage is built up by the *Thou* that is neither of the *I's*. This is the metaphysical and metapsychical factor of love to which the feelings of love are mere accompaniments."[12] "The metaphysical and metapsychical factor": what sphere have we entered upon with this feature in the situation? Is it the realm of human responsibility, a consequence of the acceptance of ethical decisions and resolutions, posited, as it were, from below, from the humanistic level? "True public and true personal life are two forms of connection. In that they come into being and endure, feelings (the changing content) and institutions (the constant form) are necessary; but put together they do not create human life: this is done by the third, the central presence of the *Thou*, or rather, more truly stated, by the central *Thou* that has been received in the present."[13] Obviously more than the Kantian understanding of the *Thou* is involved here. In one step we are carried beyond the ethical as such into what can only be called the religious. We must turn back to examine what Buber says of the *I-Thou* relation which goes beyond what we discover in Kant. There we shall find a modification of the phenomenological analysis, as it presents itself in Heidegger, with "metaphysical and metapsychical" implications of a *religious* sort: an advance, indeed, which makes it possible for one critic of Buber's thought to declare that "the social is swallowed up in the religious."[14]

Buber himself finds the real discovery of the *Thou*, in the sense in which he maintains this, in the positivist critic of Hegel, Ludwig Feuerbach (1804-72). Here, in the thinker who reduced philosophy and theology both to branches of anthropology, we find a doctrine which refuses to start off with a self-contained Subject confronting a ready-made

[12] *op. cit.*, p. 46.
[13] *ibid.*
[14] Cullberg, *Das Du und die Wirklichkeit*, p. 45.

world of Objects, and a teaching which asserts the necessity of an experience of *Thou* in order to come to consciousness of self as *I*. "The true dialectic," asserts this renegade Hegelian, "is no monologue of the isolated thinker with himself, it is a *dialogue between I and Thou*."[15] As an epistemological necessity an awareness of *Thou's* is involved in the certainty of an external world which is there not just for me but for others. Even sensuous love bears witness to the real objective otherness of a *Thou*: I cannot love what is not really other than myself and in the end an other self. Love, the criterion of reality and truth! Astonishing testimony from an atheistic positivist and materialist. Buber tells us that he himself in his youth was "given a decisive impetus by Feuerbach"; and he quotes with approval from the earlier thinker: "The individual man for himself does not have man's being in himself, either as a moral being or a thinking being. Man's being is contained only in community, in the unity of man with man—a unity which rests, however, only on the reality of the difference between I and Thou."[16]

The truth of all these positions is taken up into Buber's own doctrine of *I and Thou*. What is the development peculiar to his position? Fundamentally the advance is precisely in the teaching that in order to clarify the articulation of man's attitude to his world it is necessary to recognize *two* relations, with all that they involve, those namely of *I-It* and *I-Thou*, set alongside each other; the former essentially an epistemological relation, the latter an existential relation, and the latter the more basic, primary, inclusive, expressive of the fullness of being adequate to real life. It is doubtful whether Feuerbach really contemplated the common-sense distinction of things and persons as requiring to be transcended in any manner. In Buber *Thou's* and *It's* have interchangeable ontological status for *I's*. Man's attitude alternates between the fully existential and the merely epistemological with regard to the same elements in his world. *I-It* is the attitude of knowing, experiencing, using. *I-Thou* is the attitude of "real living," of "meeting" an "other" in a palpitating "presence" in the

[15] *Grundsätze der Philosophie der Zukunft,* 1843, p. 345; quoted Cullberg, *op. cit.,* p. 31.
[16] *Between Man and Man,* 1947, p. 147f.

"present" (for *Gegenwart* means both), of encountering a reality by which I am addressed as by an "other" of equal or greater standing or status than myself. For example, the "extended use of the *Thou*" to which we have referred above makes it possible to have a *Thou*-relation with a tree. The passage in which this is described has been called "a poem,"[17] but this does not mean that the language is to be dismissed as merely figurative; it must be taken with all philosophical seriousness. "I consider a tree. I can look on it as a picture . . . I can perceive it as movement . . . I can classify it in a species and study it as a type in its structure and mode of life . . . I can subdue its actual presence and form so sternly that I recognize it only as an expression of law . . . I can dissipate it and perpetuate it in number, in pure numerical relation . . . In all this the tree remains my object, occupies space and time, and has its nature and constitution. It can, however, also come about, if I have both will and grace, that in considering the tree I become bound up in relation to it. The tree is no longer *It*. I have been seized by the power of exclusiveness. To effect this it is not necessary for me to give up any of the ways in which I consider the tree . . . no knowledge I would have to forget. Everything belonging to the tree is in this: its form and structure, its colours and chemical composition, its intercourse with the elements and with the stars, are all present in a single whole. The tree is no impression, no play of my imagination, no value depending on my mood; but it is bodied over against me and has to do with me, as I with it—only in a different way. Let no attempt be made to sap the strength from the meaning of the relation: relation is mutual." It may be felt by the literally minded that language is here being pressed beyond what is in its power to express. On the other hand it may equally be felt that there are aspects of the real world and of real living which only such "poetry" is adequate to shadow forth. All that cool philosophy will then be able to do will be to estimate the relation of this poetry to its own prose. And here it may well be asked whether this is not just what Buber himself is trying to do in his discussions of the relations of the worlds of *It* and *Thou*. Merely in passing, we note that it would be,

[17] Leslie Paul, *op. cit.,* p. 149. *I and Thou,* p. 7f.

according to Buber, a false inference from our coming into relation with the tree to conclude that its becoming a *Thou* for us means that "the tree will have a consciousness . . . similar to our own. Of that I have no experience . . . I encounter no soul or dryad of the tree, but the tree itself."[18]

If it should still be asked: why should this encounter with a tree and analogous experiences be described in terms of the *I-Thou* relation, why this extended use of *Thou* to the non-human environment, to "our life with nature . . . with intelligible forms," why and "with what right do we draw what lies outside speech into relation with the world of the primary word" (i.e. *I-Thou*), Buber's own answer is that "the spheres in which the world of relation arises are three"— these three, life with nature, with men, with intelligible forms.[19] This answer stands in need of amplification; and here we gather together Buber's explanation from various places in *I and Thou*. "Relation" is a key word in the Buberian vocabulary: it is not an epistemological generality but bears a characteristic and specific sense in his use of it. "Relation", it turns out, is properly applicable in the case of the second primary word only, *I-Thou*. *I-It* is the relation of Subject-Object in the realm of knowledge, and not properly relation in the full sense. For knowledge is an autopsy upon the corpse of "real living," encounter or meeting in the present, a form of mutuality most clearly recognizable in the two-sided intercourse of persons when it is actually taking place. In knowledge one side of the transaction is not really active; it is dead. The Object may be "present", but we are not "in the presence" of the Object. Objects are not *present* in their own reality but *represented* in the medium of ideality, have boundaries allotted to them in time and place, are linked each to other in terms of causality, of logical necessity or natural dependence. The Subject *I* disposes of them in accordance with its own needs and purposes: they are items in a realm of being of which it is the centre. But in "real living" the circle of the Subject's being is broken into by an "other" present to it, really "there" on its own account, modifying my being and bringing me into relation, correlative action towards its own

[18] *op. cit.*, p. 8.
[19] *op. cit.*, p. 6.

being. Each is present in an unanalysed wholeness which involves distinction but no sense of boundaries or limits. Each fills all the other's firmament, and life "streams" between the two poles of the relation in mutuality, each living in the other. Buber repudiates the term "experience" in which to describe this state of affairs, "experience" belonging to the language of "objective speech" in which the Subject of knowledge is distinguished from its Objects, and which locates "experience" in the psychological realm of the "subjective," as feeling, perception, sensation and the like. This happening, then, of openness and mutuality is characteristic not only of the intercourse of persons, but of our intercourse with nature and "intelligible forms." We live in them and they in us; we are made what we are in our very being by this life of relation, so that they affect us as much as we affect them. Hence these "others" are conceived as other *I's*, i.e. as *Thou's*.

It is part of Buber's teaching that the *I-Thou* precedes *I-It*, both logically and in the history of the human consciousness. Here he makes an excursus into anthropology and linguistics. Primitive man does not clearly distinguish between himself and his environment, and his speech in full of "pre-grammatical structures (which later, splitting asunder, give rise to the many various kinds of words) mostly indicating the wholeness of a relation."[20] Only gradually does the consciousness of the unchanging partner, the *I*, sort itself out from the succession of experiences in which environment affects the man and the man the environment. "In the beginning is relation."[21] Animism and *mana* both express this primitive sense of the togetherness-in-living-relation before the separation into the living percipient man and inanimate perceived natural objects. "The first primary word can be resolved, certainly, into *I* and *Thou*, but it did not arise from their being set together; by nature it precedes the *I*. The second word arose from the setting together of *I* and *It;* by nature it comes after *I*. In the primitive relational event . . . the *I* is included . . . there are in it . . . only the two partners, the man and that which confronts him, in their full actuality, and

[20] *op. cit.,* p. 18.
[21] *loc. cit.*

. . . the man, without yet perceiving the *I* itself, is already aware of the cosmic pathos of the *I*. On the other hand the *I* is not yet included in the natural actual event which is to pass over into the primary word *I-It,* into the experience with its relation to the *I*. This actual event is the separation of the human body, as the bearer of its perceptions, from the world round about it. The body comes to know and to differentiate itself in its peculiarities . . . But when the *I* of the relation has stepped forth and taken on separate existence, it also moves, strangely tenuous and reduced to merely functional activity, into the natural, actual event of the separation of the body from the world round about it, and awakens there the state in which the *I* is properly active . . . The *I* which stepped forth declares itself to be the bearer, and the world around about to be the object, of the perceptions . . . whenever the sentence "I see the tree" is so uttered that it no longer tells of a relation between the man—*I*—and the tree—*Thou*—but establishes the perception of the tree as object by the human consciousness, the barrier between Subject and Object has been set up. The primary word *I-It,* the word of separation, has been spoken."[22] This is the natural history of the Subject-Object relation; and according to Buber, it is the story of a Fall. Knowledge, for which the Subject-Object relation is fundamental, is an expulsion from the paradise of primitive relation, in which man's blessedness is automatic, since he is together (without knowing it) with his origin and source. Henceforward relation must be consciously and continually restored or received, ever renewed and ever again lost. "Conscious life means the return of cosmic being as human becoming. Spirit appears in time as a product—even as a by-product of nature, yet it is in spirit that nature is timelessly enveloped."[23] This passage is witness that Buber's phenomenological analysis is supported by a metaphysic, and one which appears to be the presupposition rather than the consequence of his analysis. It has a strong savour, moreover, of Hegelianism. This should be remembered when we come to estimate the final validity of his construction. It should also be remembered when it is proposed to make Christian use of his

[22] *op. cit.,* p. 22f.
[23] *op. cit.,* p. 23f.

scheme, or when we take him as interpreter of biblical religion.

Knowledge being then in some sort a sickness of the soul, being always a knowledge of evil, of separation, of disruption of relation, its concepts and categories require revision in order to body forth the fullness of "real living." In particular, the associations of "objective speech" must be left behind, for the very idea of the Subject, to which *object* and *objective* are correlative, has changed. "For the *I* of the primary word *I-Thou* is a different *I* from that of the primary word *I-It* . . . Primary words are spoken from the being . . . The primary word *I-Thou* can only be spoken with the whole being. The primary word *I-It* can never be spoken with the whole being. There is no *I* taken in itself, but only the *I* of the primary word *I-Thou* and the *I* of the primary word *I-It*. When a man says *I* he refers to one or other of these. The *I* to which he refers is present when he says *I* . . . The existence of *I* and the speaking of *I* are one and the same thing. When a primary word is spoken the speaker enters the word and takes his stand in it."[24] All this, doubtless, is without prejudice to some sort of underlying unity of the *I*, the Subject, the ego. In some sense it is the same *I* which is different, according as it takes its stand in relation to *Thou* or *It*: there is no schizophrenia, for we are talking not about the psychological Subject, but about the reality which is constituted by the existential word. The Subject is no *thing*, no object with determinate boundaries in space and time. It makes itself and is made by its Object, by what is over against it, into which it enters and which enters into it. It is "life in relation," one pole (the human end) of the "streaming mutual life of the universe."[25] We have left behind here the *I* as the functional point at the centre of the synthetic unity of apperception, or even as the psychological circle described round this point as centre. The centre of this real living may well be outside the *I*. "I become through my relation to the *Thou;* as I become *I*, I say *Thou*."[26] This famous saying is even more pregnant in the original German: *"Ich werde am Du."*

[24] *op. cit.*, p. 3f.
[25] *op. cit.*, p. 16
[26] *op. cit.*, p. 11.

Here we have Existentialism in three senses, or at three levels. First, it is phenomenological analysis of "human existence" (*Existenz*) which is wider than thought. Second, it is existence brought into being by the Subject itself making itself: "The existence of *I* and the speaking of *I* are one and the same thing." And the speech is not a matter of acoustics or linguistics, but of attitude and direction of being. But third, it is also existentialism of a sort peculiarly characteristic if not altogether special to Buber, in which the *I* is made by the *Thou*. In our life with nature, with men, with intelligible forms, realized in art, religion, community, where these are alive in present actuality, we are addressed by and constituted by what is over against us, so that reality lives in us and we in reality. Incidentally, we note here a principle of evaluation, present in the recurring emphasis on *real* living, akin to Gogarten's concept of *real* history, and Heidegger's determinative concept of *authentic* human existence. Here, of course, in Buber (and in Gogarten?) it is recognized for what it is, and allowed its full weight, instead of being assimilated to pure unethical phenomenology, as in Heidegger. The question in Buber, as hinted above, is whether the ethics does not lead out into religion. But to return; Buber maintains that his form of Existentialism cannot be contained in the ontological forms of the Subject-Object relation, which is no *real* or living *relation* in the end, but only a sectional and departmental activity within the wider reality of "life in relation." Its Subject, distinguished from the objects which it articulates into a system of science linked by causal necessity, is a transcript of living reality, allowing neither for the freedom of which we are conscious nor for the reality of objects for themselves or their impact upon us. This Subject is an abstract point, a perspective viewpoint with no substance, accidentally related to its objects, unable to affect them or to be affected by them essentially. So far from the scheme of things being understandable from the putting together of ready-made subjects and objects, persons and things, *I's* and *It's*, this whole way of conceiving the universe is a late development within a richer context of existence. An ontology deriving from the Subject-Object relation taken as fundamental, must be false to the full truth, and needs to be replaced by an ontology giving full value to real life as meeting, to the new understanding of the *Thou*, which in turn throws new light upon the *I*. We do not first establish knowledge and then read off what life and reality are permitted to be. Knowledge is itself a function of life, and a limited one at that, with a tendency to distort the parent relation—with an impulse indeed to patri- or matricide!

May it not be that the sense of liberation which many have felt come upon them from acquaintance with Buber's book derives precisely from this feature of his construction? There is a feeling that the tyranny of an age-old misunderstanding of "objectivity" has at last been decisively broken; that the intangibles of community with nature, man and God can no longer be dismissed as "merely subjective" fancies in the soul of man, but have their legitimate place in the interpretation of the nature of things, are a very revelation of reality. Consider this passage from Leslie Paul: "Buber's argument . . . is that with objects we have an It relationship—we address them as It—and this Subject-Object relationship implies one consciousness examining or appropriating a world of objects in the being of which it does not share. They are *other*. But a *Thou* relationship, more truly an *I-Thou* relationship, cannot belong at the same time to the *I-It* class, for it is not a Subject-Object relation at all, but a *meeting*. It is useless (argues Buber) to apply the term "objective" to the *I-It* relation and "subjective" to the *I-Thou* meeting for there is a real sense in which nothing could be further from the truth. In the *I-It* relationship nothing could be more subjective than the existence of a single realizing subject cut off from the objects it is experiencing by the barrier of difference in kind or incongruity of approach, and in the *I-Thou* relationship nothing could be more objective than the meeting of like beings in the territory between them. If once we grasp the tremendous import of this idea, so profound and so simple, it cannot but change our understanding and our lives."[27]

It is an old truism that nothing is altered by changing its name; and new definitions of "subjective" and "objective" will effect no changes in the structure of knowledge or

[27] *The Meaning of Human Existence,* p. 148f.

reality. Surely the moral of this passage is either (a) that the terms "subjective" and "objective" are merely misleading in the context of the "Buberian" ontology, or (b) these terms are not tied (as Buber's discussion suggests they are tied) to their associations in the Subject-Object relation of knowledge. Can we get rid of "objectivity" as the value of "truth" in knowledge? When Buber polemizes against knowledge, must it not be against knowledge in a special sense? His statements about the insight into the nature of reality gained in *I-Thou* encounter, if they are not to be left in the unenviable position of being statements about which no discussion is possible, must themselves be either true or false, valid or invalid. And since the opposite of truth is error—an opposite whose possibility is posited in the bare conception of truth—can we get rid of "subjectivity" as one source of error? Psychologically considered, error occurs objectively as subjective fact: it is "real" enough, in all conscience! In this use of the terms "subjective" and "objective" both true and false ideas are equally both subjective and objective. Truth is a value, not a psychological occurrence. But this does not argue anything inherently wrong in the Subject-Object relation, in such knowledge as is open to human finitude. Knowledge is a "trans-subjective relation" to an object, namely, reality. Thus truth and error posit their own definitions of Subject and Object, whatever be our formula for the nature of knowledge, whether correspondence or coherence. Buber laments the exalted melancholy of our fate that every *Thou* in our world must become an *It*. This may or may not be tragic. The fact remains that all discussion, even discussion of *I-Thou* and *I-It* attitudes, and of the disclosure in every particular *Thou* of an *eternal Thou* (to which we have still to come in our treatment), all this must be discussed in speech as a branch of knowledge; and of all discussion the living concern is an answer to the question: Is this true? not just: Does this occur? No conceivable transposition or modification of the use of the terms "subjective" and "objective" will exempt us from the onerous and difficult attempt upon this question of truth.

Sometimes Buber speaks of the realm of relation as that of *between*. Thus, treating of love, he is anxious to distinguish the ontological reality of love from that of the feelings which accompany it. "Feelings accompany the metaphysical and metapsychical fact of love, but they do not constitute it. . . . Feelings are "entertained": love comes to pass. Feelings dwell in man; but man dwells in his love. That is no metaphor, but the actual truth. Love does not cling to the *I* in such a way as to have the *Thou* only for its 'content,' its object; but love is *between I* and *Thou*."[28] Again: "Feelings are a mere accompaniment to the metaphysical and metapsychical fact of the relation, which is fulfilled not in the soul but between the *I* and *Thou*." And later in the same paragraph there is mention of "an isolated and limited feeling . . . a relative psychological matter."[29] The two references to "metaphysical and metapsychical fact" are interesting. The realm of relation is "beyond" (*meta*) both matter (physics) and soul (psyche), and this realm is "between" *I* and *Thou*, which in their turn are not "psychological matters." And this language, furthermore, is not *"meta*phor." All language, however, being inherently metaphorical it so happens that "beyond" and "between" are themselves spatial metaphors. This does not signify that the matters referred to are themselves merely metaphorical. But it does suggest that language is here being strained somewhat beyond its literal limits, if not indeed to express the inexpressible. It will definitely not do to hypostatize the realm of "between" as if it were a quasi-physical locus of relation: that would be a lapse into "objective speech," which "snatches only at a fringe of real life."[30] But when Buber insists that relation, meeting, love are "not fulfilled in the soul" does he seriously suggest that knowledge (which is depreciated in comparison with these features of "real living") is itself "fulfilled" in the soul? The acts and processes of knowledge take place in a psychological Subject, which has a history in time and space, whose experiences can be made the object of a special science. But in knowledge the self is open to and in touch with a reality beyond itself, and the judgements it makes have a trans-subjective reference to which the valua-

[28] *op. cit.,* p. 14f.
[29] *op. cit.,* p. 81.
[30] *op. cit.,* p. 17.

tion of truth or error can be attached. Knowledge itself is a "metapsychical fact" with "metaphysical" implications. It has not hitherto been thought necessary to postulate a special dimension of reality in which truth may dwell—except perhaps in poetical and rhetorical exercises. It is enough to be warned of the dangers of "psychologism." Is the difference between knowledge and the life of relation, of which Buber treats, so great as to constitute a difference in kind, requiring a special ontological dimension in which community, mutuality, meeting and the rest may be lodged secure from the assaults of "objective speech" and objective thinking? Do not the relations of knowledge to the existential realities of relation, to "real living," in short, require to be matter of further thought and determination? Their haven of refuge must lie under no suspicion of being perchance a no-man's-land—still less cloud-cuckoo-land.

It is no resolution of the question of the "objectivity" (in the sense of the ultimate truth) of the *I-Thou* experiences—what else are we to call them, in spite of Buber's objections to the term "experience"?—to say that they have their reality in their simple happening. Most certainly they happen to those to whom they do happen! But insanity, hallucinations, errors also happen, as psychological fact. Buber is right in insisting that reality in the full sense is not simply identical with occurrence in this fashion. What he says in condemnation of "objective speech" we should say tends to ignore the trans-subjective reference of knowledge, the truth-value which is not a matter of psychological fact or happening. On the other hand there *is* a sense in which the *I-Thou* relational life must or should guarantee its own objectivity or truth. By the nature of its mere happening it should reveal itself as intrinsic reality. The note of authenticity, moreover, should not be a matter of feeling exhausting itself in such a judgement as "This is marvellous! It is good for us to be here." Along with the exaltation there must be a disclosure of reality, which brings its own authentication, certainly, but which also declares its relevance to other perspectives upon reality. An *I-Thou* relation contains many elements of mediation in solution, as Buber has himself declared. In such a relation with a tree we remember that it was said that no kind of knowledge of the tree was left behind, not even its chemical constitution.[31] And such relations as we may have with the tree in immediacy of meeting are possible with everything and anything in the world, or with the whole round world itself in one. Unless we are content to say that, as and when they occur, all such relations are equally true for the *I* to which they occur, then we must seek some other criterion of truth than mere occurrence. The relation must throw some light upon its elements, in its own or in other contexts. It must be significant or revelatory. Otherwise all such occurrences are all equally real and equally trivial, globules of immediacy threaded like beads upon a string.

"Revelatory"! Certainly Buber intends the *I-Thou* relation as revelation: a double revelation, indeed. A revelation of the true nature of things which degrades "objective knowledge" to a mere scratching at the outside of things, compared with a knowledge which penetrates to their essence; but also a revelation which shows the cosmos as truly *Thou*, seeking to have to do with the *I*, to make him by entering into relation with him, or by inviting him to enter into relation with itself. The ultimate nature of things is a dialogue between man and the cosmos. Whether the further doctrine of Buber that every particular *Thou* is an emanation or breath of an eternal *Thou* is to be interpreted theistically or pantheistically is a question which we postpone meantime. Our present concern is with whether the aspect of things as *Thou* at all is projection from man's side, the result of his "attitude" to them, or represents a real feature of *their* nature, essence or character. Buber certainly intends this last. He applies in this connection the theological concept of "grace." "The *Thou* meets me through grace— it is not found through seeking."[32] Grace does not destroy the need for action on my part: whether the *I-Thou* relationship goes further than invitation and possibility depends on me. "My speaking of the primary word to it is an act of my being, is indeed *the*

---

[31] Query: is that knowledge present consciously in the *I-Thou* relation with the tree? Is it not rather that the *I-Thou* relation and *I-It* relation need not, should not on explication, contradict each other's deliverances?

[32] *op. cit.*, p. 11.

act of my being. The *Thou* meets me. But I step into direct
relation with it. Hence the relation means being chosen and
choosing, suffering and action in one."[33] Buber's is not intended as an Existentialism which makes the Subject wholly
responsible for his universe, which pictures the Subject as saying "I make my own world, create my own Object and objectivity: this, at any rate, is what the world means to me. I take
full responsibility for my own private construction of meaning and value in things, and to that extent they are real."
Buber does not intend an objectivity on these terms: there is a
meaning in things which is revealed in the accepted invitation to the *I-Thou* relation. Even in my encounter with the
tree this last "is no impression, no play of my imagination, no
value depending upon my mood; but it is bodied over against
me and has to do with me, as I with it—only in a different
way."[34] The world makes me in its address to me, in its
meeting with me. Not in its mere moulding of me in causal
necessity, in my heredity, my place in my nation and my
station in society. When I say *Thou* to these things, to these
concrete historical determinations of my being, they become
not just fate but destiny. They are life *meeting* me with a
particular face and set of features and challenging me to a
particular response in freedom. The living, satisfying quality
of such life in relation, compared with life at second-hand
in received attitudes or in the shelter of social institutions, or
in the escape from life in empty isolation or the cult of
"personality," which turns out to be the mere indulgence of
idiosyncrasy—this vitality must in the end be self-evidencing
in its value, and in that sense its own guarantee of its
"objectivity" or "truth." The life of relation is not a truth or
objectivity that can be established or disproved by knowledge
identified with the scientific attitude. If it is a revelation of the
meaning of the universe it is a truth not independent of the
will and purpose to enter into such meaning, hinted at if not
plainly disclosed by life itself.

To ask for a "proof" or "objective" justification of this
revelation on grounds which cut out this element of risk, of
venturing existence upon its practical truth, is perhaps to ask

[33] *ibid.*
[34] *op. cit.*, p. 8.

for the impossible. Perhaps all attempt upon the truth of reality as it is in itself and for itself, apart from the human grasp upon it both of knowledge and action, is a mistaken adventure. Perhaps it is only in such taking up into human knowledge and action that the meaningless welter of mere brute existence receives meaning, direction, significance. But behind Buber's position is the conviction that somehow this very development is "intended" by the nature of things, is an ultimate meaning behind apparent meaninglessness of mere happening. There is so much meaning up to a point in nature—its law, order, rationality—that mankind seems incapable of really believing that it all means nothing, that reality does not really approach us with an invitation to its own completion, is not in fact a greater *Thou* addressing us in a speech that will hint where it does not openly state, coax where it will not command, invite where it will not compel. Whether all this can be held apart from something like a definitely theistic interpretation of the universe is another matter. Whether it can be held on a pantheistic view of the universe, short of theism which posits some sort of conscious purposiveness at the heart of the universe, is (as we have already said) a crux in the interpretation and evaluation of Buber's scheme. But it is perhaps a mistaken search to look for an objective verification of Buber's position in some sort of phenomenological inevitability about his extension of the *Thou* to cover non-personal reality as that meets us in apparent address. Can such analysis really go beyond the certainty of human address, of man's saying *Thou* to nature? Can it ever deliver us from the lingering doubt whether nature's *Thou* to man be more than an instance of "the pathetic fallacy"? It may be certain that man, in the higher reaches of his spiritual being—nay, even in the fulfilment of his natural relations as father, food producer, social being —is made by his relation with the natural and human environment out of which he springs. Yet all this is less than saying that environment sets about doing so: the *Thou* of nature may be the reflection of man's taking to do with it, rather than its seriously taking to do with him. *I and Thou* has been called a "philosophical-religious poem,"[35] "a collec-

[35] E. T., "Intro." p. vi

tion of aphorisms, partly in the form of poetry."[36] What may
be inconclusive as phenomenological analysis may yet be
highly moving and even convincing as poetry. After all, one
of our own poets has said things strikingly like Buber.

> "I have felt
> A presence that disturbs me with the joy
> Of elevated thoughts; a sense sublime
> Of something far more deeply interfused,
> Whose dwelling is the light of setting suns,
> And the round ocean and the living air,
> And the blue sky, and in the mind of man."

A "presence"—*Gegenwart,* the sense of *Thou;* "before the
face," "in the Presence," these are Buber's very language,[37]
speaking, of course, about the explicit *religious* situation or
sense of the eternal *Thou.* Even the ambiguity of the status
of *Thouness* in environment we can find hinted at in Wordsworth:

> "All the mighty world
> Of eye and ear—both what they half create,
> And what perceive."

The doctrine of approach and address to man, of what
Buber calls the feature of "grace" in the dialogue of man
and cosmos, this too can be found in the same poet:

> "Nor less I deem that there are Powers
> Which of themselves our minds impress;
> That we can feed this mind of ours
> In a wise passiveness.
> Think you 'mid all this mighty sum
> Of things for ever speaking,
> That nothing of itself will come,
> But we must still be seeking"?

Such an essentially religious view of life can still be maintained short of translating the eternal *Thou* of Buber and the

[36] Cullberg, *op. cit.,* p. 40.
[37] *op. cit.,* pp. 83, 95.

"presences and powers" of Wordsworth into actual *personality* in a theistic God, no doubt (with ultimate justification, however, only with considerable doubt). It would certainly be the final justification of Buber's position, the ultimate guarantee of the "objectivity" of his system, if it concluded to and were concluded in a view of the universe as grounded in divine personality. Such a coalescence of philosophy and poetry would justify, too, Wordsworth's view of poetry as "the breath and finer spirit of all knowledge." There is considerable doubt whether Buber is to be so interpreted, however. And to a detailed consideration of this matter we must now turn, as the last topic in our discussion and treatment of *I and Thou*.

From the "exalted melancholy of our fate, that every *Thou* in our world must become an *It*," one reality alone, according to Martin Buber, is excepted. "The eternal *Thou* can by its nature not become *It;* for by its nature it cannot be established in measure and bounds, not even in the measure of the immeasurable, or the bounds of boundless being; for by its nature it cannot be understood as a sum of qualities, nor even as an infinite sum of qualities raised to a transcendental level; for it can be found neither in nor out of the world; for it cannot be experienced or thought; for we miss Him, Him who is, if we say 'I believe that He is'—'He' is also a metaphor, but 'Thou' is not."[38] This eternal *Thou* is the reality whom men call God, and this name is "most imperishable and most indispensable."[39] If God cannot be expressed He can always be addressed. The name does not matter. "For he who speaks the word God and really has *Thou* in mind . . . addresses the true *Thou* of his life, which cannot be limited by another *Thou*, and to which he stands in a relation that gathers up and includes all others."[40] "The extended lines of relations meet in the eternal *Thou*. Every particular *Thou* is a glimpse through to the eternal *Thou*; by means of every particular *Thou* the primary word addresses the eternal *Thou*. Through this mediation of the *Thou* of all beings fulfilment, and non-fulfilment, of relations comes to

[38] *op. cit.,* p. 112.
[39] *loc. cit.*
[40] *op. cit.,* p. 75f.

them."[41] "The *Thou* of all beings"; that is as near as we shall
get to a definition of the "eternal *Thou*" in Martin Buber.
God is the source of *Thouness* in the universe, *is* "the streaming life of the universe" as speech, address to beings capable
of hearing and speaking in their turn; and all particular cases
of encounter, of that meeting in which real life consists, are
calls to enter directly into relation with the *Thou* which
occasions them at our particular junctures of space, time
and circumstance, indirectly with the *Thou* which is in them
all, includes them all, but is not in turn included in the
totality of them. "God comprises, but is not, the universe."[42]

Buber specifically repudiates mysticism, as the end of all
life of true relation, because it destroys the essential and
abiding duality of encounter or meeting. These are valuable
pages in the third part of his little book, in which he shows
the Johannine tradition in New Testament thought to be
non-mystical but essentially "the Gospel of pure relation."[43]
But something like what popular usage means by mysticism
seems present in the immediacy with which in Buber's
representation the eternal *Thou* inheres in the particular
Thou's, in the immediacy also with which human beings
establish contact with this eternal *Thou,* in the varied
instances of meeting or encounter. "Through each process of
becoming that is present to us we look out toward the
fringe of the eternal *Thou;* in each *Thou* we address the
eternal *Thou*."[44] "To step into pure relation is not to disre-
gard everything, but to see everything in the *Thou,* not to re-
nounce the world but to establish it on its true basis . . . he
who sees the world in God stands in His presence."[45] This
position is not argued to by Buber, but simply stated as the
obvious implication of awareness of the *Thou*. "God cannot
be inferred in anything—in nature, say, as its author, or in
history as its master, or in the subject as the self that is
thought in it. Something else is not 'given' and God then
elicited from it; but God is the Being that is most directly,

[41] *ibid.*
[42] *op. cit.,* p. 95.
[43] *op. cit.,* p. 85.
[44] *op. cit.,* p. 101.
[45] *op. cit.,* p. 79.

most nearly, and lastingly, over against us, that may properly only be addressed, not expressed."[46] "The world of *It* is set in the context of space and time. The world of *Thou* is not set in the context of either of these. Its context is in the centre, where the extended lines of relation meet—in the eternal *Thou*."[47] The "context of the *Thou*": God is as near, as universal, as obvious (or not obvious!) as that! "He who goes out with his whole being to meet his *Thou* and carries to it all being that is in the world, finds Him who cannot be sought . . . God is the mystery of the self-evident, nearer to me than my I."[48] We remember that "the separated I" is the product of reflective distinction operating upon primitive togetherness-in-relation.

What then is involved in the position, strenuously contested by Buber, that this eternal *Thou* can never suffer the fate of the particular *Thou's* in which it manifests itself, and can never become an *It*? Obviously, two things at least are intended: God, as the eternal *Thou*, can never become a particular, one amongst other objects in a catalogue of known or knowable realities; and secondly, God is not an Object in the dispassionate knowledge relation of Subject and Object, He is known in existential encounter involving the whole being, the "inborn Thou" finding its counterpart in the *Thou* of all *Thou's*.

First: God is not a particular. This would be widely conceded—even insisted upon—apart from Buber's special reading of the meaning of the proposition. Scholasticism can talk of God as a universal, or as *the* Universal. When religion is aware of its own nature it agrees that God is not just one amongst others—certainly not just one thing amongst other things, even where His nature is allowed to be spirit. He is not one item in His universe. He is not even *primus inter pares*. Such an object is not that with which religion feels it has to do. "In face of what the archetypal word 'God' means, rational criticism is powerless. In face of an objectively existing God, atheism is right."[49] So Paul Tillich, who

[46] *op. cit.*, p. 80f.
[47] *op. cit.*, p. 100.
[48] *op. cit.*, p. 79.
[49] *The Interpretation of History*, 1936, p. 47.

in this connection can speak well of Nietzsche, and indicates his own borrowing of the term "archetypal words" from Martin Buber. *I and Thou* in effect tells us we do not need to climb up into heaven to find God in the form of a "magnified, non-natural man." "I know nothing of a 'world' and a 'life in the world' that might separate a man from God."[50] The world of sense does not need to be laid aside . . . no 'going beyond sense-experience' is necessary; for every experience, even the most spiritual, could yield us only an *It*."[51] God is no possible Object of sense-experience in a Subject-Object relation of knowledge. "Nor is any recourse necessary to a world of ideas or values; for they cannot become presentness for us."[52] (Does this mean that "ideas or values" cannot become *Gegenwart* as *Thou's* for us; or that they cannot be present as objects of sensuous perception, as things?) " 'Here world, there God' is the language of *It*: 'God in the world' is another language of *It*."[53] "The world in God" is only saved from being still more language of *It* for Buber, because the world is found in God as *Thou*. This brings us to the second point.

God, or the eternal *Thou,* is never known as *It,* because He is not known in the Subject-Object relation of knowledge or experience, but only in the *Thou* of existential encounter. What is or may be known or spoken of God out of such relation is not the Godness of God, so to speak, or God as God, but something else—theology, maybe, reflection upon, recollection of, what was known of God when we stood in the Presence or before the Face, in the presentness (*Geganwart*) of encounter or meeting (*Begegnung*). That this position, too, has come to be acceptable in many quarters is measure of the influence of Buber in recent theological discussion. The theology which used to call itself "dialectical" started out with a heavy indebtedness here. As an indication of its influence elsewhere take this from Paul Tillich. "Attempts to elaborate a theology as an empirical-inductive or a metaphysical-deductive 'science,' or as a combination of

50 *op. cit.,* p. 95.
51 *op. cit.,* p. 77.
52 *ibid.*
53 *op. cit.,*.p. 79.

both, have given evidence that no such attempt can succeed. In every assumedly scientific theology there is a point where individual experience, traditional valuation and personal commitment must decide the issue . . . If an inductive approach is employed . . . an *a priori* of experience and valuation is implied. The same is true of a deductive approach . . . the ultimate principles in idealist theology are rational expressions of an ultimate concern; like all metaphysical ultimates, they are religious ultimates at the same time . . . In both the empirical and the metaphysical approaches . . . the *a priori* which directs the induction and the deduction is a type of mystical experience . . . an immediate experience of something ultimate in value and being of which one can become intuitively aware. Idealism and naturalism . . . both are dependent on a point of identity between the experiencing subject and the ultimate which appears in religious experience or in the experience of the world as 'religious' . . . a 'mystical *a priori*,' an awareness of something which transcends the cleavage between subject and object . . . Every understanding of spiritual things is circular . . . if in the course of a 'scientific' procedure this *a priori* is discovered, its discovery is possible only because it was present from the very beginning."[54] This is true, according to Tillich, of the Christian theology and theologian. "He adds to the 'mystical *a priori*' the criterion of the Christian message . . . He enters the theological circle with a concrete commitment. He enters it as a member of the Christian church to perform one of the essential functions of the Church—its theological self-interpretation."[55] "Personal commitment" here corresponds to Buber's "going out to meet the *Thou*": the "mystical *a priori*," although Buber repudiates the term "mysticism," corresponds to the immediacy of our knowledge of the ultimate *Thou*, and the immanence of this in particular *Thou's*. The "something ultimate of which one can become intuitively aware" of Tillich is in Buber the eternal *Thou*; and this ultimate, known in encounter and commitment, is in the meeting itself, in presentness, something which "transcends the cleavage between subject and

[54] Tillich, *Systematic Theology*, Nisbet, Vol. I, 1953, p. 11f.
[55] Tillich, *loc. cit.*

object." Whatever this may mean, such awareness is not the knowledge of a passive object by an active subject, both limited and self-contained entities on either side. It is not an *It* which I distinguish from my own ego as such, and which I dispose of for my own ends as if it had no beings and rights for and of itself.

And yet Buber has to concede that in certain circumstances and for certain purposes the eternal *Thou*—like the particular *Thou's*—has to be treated, not altogether illegitimately, as an *It*! The knowledge relation returns, and with it some sort of distinction between Subject and Object, in *theology*, where God is an object of thought, distinguishable from other objects of thought. Besides speaking to God and hearing Him speak (grant this meantime!), men must also speak about God. The beginnings of such objectification lie within "religion" itself. How so? "How do the Presence and the power received by men in revelation change into a 'content'?"[56] It appears that man cannot always live and act "in the Presence" or "before the Face." He must come down from the mount of meeting and transact his daily life and business on the plain. "Presentness" we cannot hold; we must draw breath and pass to something else, being creatures of time and becoming. But "man desires to possess God; he desires a continuity in space and time of possession of God. He is not content with the inexpressible confirmation of meaning, but wants to see this confirmation stretched out as something that can be continually taken up and handled, a continuum unbroken in space and time that insures his life at every point and every moment."[57] Continuity in time is secured by turning God into an object of *faith*, which at first completes, then gradually comes to replace the acts of relation. "Resting in belief in an *It* takes the place of the continually renewed movement of the being towards concentration and going out to the relation."[58] Extension in space is secured when the religious man unites himself in a community of the faithful, and "thus God becomes the

[56] *op. cit.*, p. 113.
[57] *loc. cit.*
[58] *loc. cit.*

object of a cult."[59] Both faith and community (or Church) thus appear, if not regrettable, at least dangerous necessities in religion. For "pure relation," by which Buber designates specific orientation towards the eternal *Thou,* "can only be raised to constancy in space and time by being embodied in the whole stuff of life."[60] In passing we may note that in Buber faith is not contrasted with sight: we do not endure as seeing Him who is invisible in this present life. Rather we endure as remembering Him whom we have recently encountered and hope soon again to encounter face to face— God being, as we have already seen, "the Being that is most directly, most nearly, most lastingly, over against us," the Presence in presentness (*Gegenwart*).

We may perhaps allow that Buber has maintained his real point. God Himself is spoken *of* in theology and religion, in "the expressed knowledge and ordered action of the religions."[61] But God Himself is not entangled in such speech: "He" being a metaphor, but "Thou" not. How much less has God submitted to be found as an "It," an Object which can appear to a Subject! Whatever can be argued to or about in such dispassionate speech is at any rate not God— is He not the existential reality that can be found in meeting to which we go out when we speak the primary word *Thou* with our whole being? The "expressed knowledge and ordered action of the religions" are secondary, not primary, phenomena in religion. They presuppose that we have been in the Presence, and they involve and imply that we are no longer there. God is, and is known, only in existential encounter, where the *Thou* fills our firmament, and there is no room to stand apart and look upon an *It,* where only life streams between *I* and *Thou.* Buber's account of faith and cult and church are suggestive, and cover much of the ground on any account of religion. But there is a remaining doubt on what, to most of us, must seem an all-important matter.

In the passage just quoted from Tillich's *Systematic Theology* the ultimate is spoken of as that "which appears in religious experience or in the experience of the world as

[59] *op. cit.,* p. 114.
[60] *loc. cit.*
[61] *op. cit.,* p. 112.

'religious.' "[62] Is the ultimate which Martin Buber designates "the eternal *Thou*" in the end "the world as religiously experienced"? In spite of the personalistic complexion of his position and exposition, is the religion of *I and Thou* not unfairly to be described as Pantheism?

There is no need at this late stage for multifarious quotation to the effect that this eternal *Thou* is met with in the world and only in the world, in the particular *Thou's* encountered in the actual world known to us. But is there any hint that the eternal *Thou* exists for and of itself, is conscious Spirit which purposes encounter with other finite spirits which have put in their appearance in the course of the world's becoming, in the history of the evolution of Spirit? "Creation reveals, in meeting, its essential nature as form,"[63] and "Form's silent asking, man's loving speech, the mute proclamation of the creature, all are gates leading into the presence of the Word. But when the full and complete meeting is to take place, the gates are united in one gateway of real life, and you no longer know through which you have entered."[64] Again: "His (*sc.* man's) sense of *Thou*, which cannot be satiated till he finds the endless *Thou*, had the *Thou* present to it from the beginning; the presence had only to become wholly real to him in the hallowed life of the world."[65] "The hallowed life of the world" is not far from "the world religiously experienced." "Form's silent asking, man's loving speech": does not that suggest that it is man who says *Thou* to a revelation which is never vocal of itself but waits on man's discovery that this eternal *Thou* had been there from the beginning? "God comprises, but is not, the universe."[66] God and the universe are not identical *simpliciter,* for Buber; but God is the universe speaking to man, met by man under the form (projected or reflected image?) of his own nature as *Thou,* the eternal *Thou* in whom the extended lines of all encounter relations meet. But while man can indeed say *Thou* to God, and in so doing finds "real

[62] *op. cit.,* p. 12.
[63] *op. cit.,* p. 26.
[64] *op. cit.,* p. 102.
[65] *op. cit.,* p. 80.
[66] *op. cit.,* p. 95.

life," does God in very deed say *Thou* to man? The discovery of the *Thou* is made by each man in the particulars of his own destiny, in his place in historical time and place, in his race, station and its duties, in the chances (what else can they be?) of his contacts with nature, man, and intelligible forms. In the sense that he did not make himself or choose his place in the context of space and time, in the sense that his life is given him and prescribed by the all-embracing life of the universe, the universe in turn may be conceived as addressing him, summoning him to speak the word which will call form out of brute fact. But these occasions have not been sharpened to a point to pierce his spirit broad awake by any particular providence. God is not a particular purpose, and it remains doubtful whether He is at all "particular" whether or not his speech is heard and replied to by men. His speech is indeed hardly to be distinguished from silence —"form's silent asking," "the mute proclamation of the creature." As for a particular revelation! Well, there is talk of "the eternal revelation that is present here and now . . . I do not believe in a self-naming of God, a self-definition of God before men. The Word of revelation is *I am that I am*. That which reveals is that which reveals. That which is *is*, and nothing more. The eternal source of strength streams, the eternal contact persists, the eternal voice sounds forth, and nothing more."[67] Shall we marvel if there are those who are reminded by this quotation from the Bible less of Buber's descent from Abraham, Isaac and Moses than of his racial kinship with Benedict Spinoza? Is "the streaming life of the universe," which catches man up into converse with itself, the "living God" of the Bible? Could such a God draw near, having heard the cry of His afflicted people in Egypt, and speak to Moses out of the burning bush of Sinai? Cullberg is of the opinion that Buber's endeavour to escape the objectification of God as a particular, to prevent God's being found one thing amongst others by finding God in all things and funding all things back into God, results in "a concept of God of so pantheistic a ring" that one not only is reminded of Spinoza, but also recollects with new force the motto on the title-page of *I and Thou* from "the old pagan"

[67] *op. cit.*, p. 111f.

Goethe: "So, waiting, I have won you from the end: God's presence in each element."[68]

Consider, in conclusion, this passage from the last pages of the "great little book": "The two primary metacosmical movements of the world—expansion into its own being and reversal to connection—find their supreme human form . . . in the history of the human relation to God. In reversal the Word is born on earth, in expansion the Word enters the chrysalis form of religion, in fresh reversal it is born again with new wings."[69] "The two primary metacosmical movements of the world": "the world" is the more fundamental term with Buber than "God." History of the cosmos is his theme; and we have already remarked on the Hegelian accent and reminiscence. Buber comes to rest in a final Binity of the cosmos, not a Trinity of Godhead. According to the primary words man speaks he enters upon existence in a world of *It* or of *Thou*; and this choice of possibilities is grounded in a metaphysical and metacosmical duality of movement in the ultimate nature of things. A great deal is said about God's need of us, besides our need of God. "There is a becoming of the God that is. The world is not divine sport, it is divine destiny. There is divine meaning in the life of the world, of man, of human persons, of you and of me . . . God needs you, for the very meaning of your life."[70] This language may conceivably leave the door open for a being of God for Himself. On the other hand it also suggests a supreme equivocation on the crucial question: who needs whom? In the end, is Buber merely an existentialist veneer upon Hegel?

[68] Cullberg, *op. cit.*, p. 45.
[69] *op. cit.*, p. 116.
[70] *op. cit.*, p. 82.

Chapter 6

God "Indissolubly Subject"

Karl Barth

A CATCHWORD WHICH occurs frequently in modern theological discussion speaks of God as "the Subject who is never Object." This usage probably stems from Martin Buber, and covers in part those matters we discussed at the end of the last chapter: God is not a particular that can be presented among the particular objects of knowledge, and furthermore He is not an object of dispassionate knowledge at all, but the reality over against us in the encounter of real living challenging to commitment. Buber talks rarely of God as "Subject"; but he is concerned to deny that God is "Object"; for this word belongs to the knowledge relation, and suggests what is passively present to the senses and is at the disposal of that science which murders to dissect. God is the eternal *Thou* which cannot become an *It*—with what reservations we have already seen. The phrase "the Subject who is never Object" is therefore not his. The formula is probably more often applied to denote certain similar trains of thought in the theology of Karl Barth. It is doubtful if the formula occurs here either. It trembles on the verge of utterance in such a passage as this: "The Subject of revelation (*sc.* God) is the Subject that remains indissolubly Subject. We cannot get behind this Subject. It cannot become an object."[1] Barth talks a great deal about God as "Subject," "indissolubly Subject." But he very definitely allows that God is in certain respects "Object," if not "an object." God is Object to His own self-knowledge in the life of the eternal Trinity, Object of faith-knowledge to man in revelation, a disclosure which in turn presents God as Subject, the living Lord who calls

[1] *The Doctrine of the Word of God,* T. & T. Clark, E. T. of Barth's *Kirchliche Dogmatik,* I. 1, p. 438. Quotations from this volume of the *Dogmatik* are made from this translation, 1936.

for man's obedience, the active Subject in originating man's knowledge of Himself, both as to its form and its matter, its possibility and its substance. Indeed, Subject and Object are very ready in Barth to collapse into each other in a way that suggests careful definition is necessary in each context. When we say that for Barth the subjectivity of God (i.e. God's *Subjektsein*, being Subject) is the guarantee of the objectivity of the Christian revelation and its truth, some measure of the ambivalence of his terminology is indicated. The influence of other usages than the purely epistemological one of the Subject-Object relation in the Kantian sense needs to be taken into account, particularly the grammatical senses of subject, predicate and object, together with the common-sense metaphysics they imply. But although somewhat various in its implications Barth's usage is extremely subtle; and the fullness and detail of his exposition make it worth while, whatever one's attitude to his theology as a whole, to examine this at some length, as the final stage in our tracing the vagaries of the Subject-Object terminology in modern theology. And one further point must be made in these preliminaries, showing *inter alia* the need for discriminating his position over against Martin Buber's. Being the remains of a good Kantian, Barth never suggests that the Subject-Object relation of knowledge is in this life to be superseded by some superior mode of insight. God Himself is Subject and Object in relation, as Father, Son and Holy Spirit; and therein lies the possibility of the divine Subject's making Himself Object to man's faith in the life of the Holy Spirit in man's soul. Perhaps certain elements in the Kantian epistemology are responsible for some questionable features in Barth, in his account of what the human Subject can and cannot do in knowing God. At any rate, the Subject-Object relation is not done away in faith, neither is there any psychological displacing of the human Subject by the divine Subject in revelation, or in the appropriation of revelation worked by the Holy Spirit in man's heart and mind. Faith-knowledge is still knowledge. There is no disparagement of the knowledge relation as such, no talk of its being a misfortune, an "exalted melancholy of our fate." We are indeed expelled from paradise; but not by the constitution of our finite human nature as such. Human knowledge is corrupted by the disobedience of sin, by the original sin of *pride,* that would be as gods, knowing for and by ourselves, instead of from and through God only, who is Truth. What the Christian hope points to in paradise regained is that we shall know as also we are known. The "knowledge which shall vanish away" is knowledge "in part" contrasted with "that which is perfect."[2]

God is known by man in encounter as *Thou,* in an existential situation, which is on one side human response, depends upon man's entering into relation: He cannot be known "merely objectively," as an item in any kind of disinterested, dispassionate knowledge, whether scientific, historical, metaphysical—He is not an Object in that sense at all. This position Barth shares with Buber.[3] But Barth knows this God with complete objectivity because all that he says and believes about Him derives from one altogether particular revelation of Himself, a "self-definition of God before men" such as Buber denies having any knowledge of,[4] which the living God of the Bible has made in the event called Jesus Christ, a revelation "from faith to faith." Never was dogmatics more self-consciously set within the "theological circle" of which Paul Tillich speaks. "Theology is a function of the Church . . . the scientific test to which the Christian Church puts herself regarding the language about God which is peculiar to her."[5] This is the language of committed faith. "To be in the Church means to be called upon with others through Jesus Christ. To act in the Church means to act in obedience to this call. This obedience to the call of Christ is faith. In faith the judgement of God is acknowledged and

---

[2] cf. *Kirchliche Dogmatik,* II. 1, p. 46.

[3] cf. the passage quoted from *Church Dogmatics,* I. 1, p. 438. From now on *Church Dogmatics* or *Kirchliche Dogmatik* will be omitted from references; I. 1 means the English translation, *The Doctrine of the Word of God,* 1936 (unless otherwise indicated) and the untranslated volumes of the *Kirchliche Dogmatik* will be referred to by their numbers in the German original, i.e. I.2 and II.1, which are all that concern us here.

[4] *I and Thou,* p. 112.

[5] I.1.1.

His grace praised."[6] The speech of Christian theology is therefore not unfairly to be described (not that Barth himself so describes it) as phenomenological analysis of an existential situation, namely, the encounter of faith with the supreme *Thou* (this language is Barth's, as we have already said and shall shortly see), with the God who reveals Himself in Jesus Christ sovereign Lord, Reconciler, and Redeemer. What remains doubtful in Buber is here resolved *ab initio*. God exists for Himself, is active in the fullest sense in encounter, takes the initiative and maintains the sovereign position in His approach to man, speaks the first and the last word in this intercourse by which a man is made over again, a new creation in Christ Jesus.[7] All that the Church knows about God depends upon this initiative of God, upon what He has told her about Himself, upon His speaking which she has heard and answered. The primary word is not a word which man speaks to his world, making it either *It* or *Thou*. It is the Word of God, which was in the beginning with God, and was God, and through whom all things were made. This Word, revealed in Jesus Christ, written in Holy Scripture, preached in the Church's message; coming forth from the Father, taking flesh in the Son, appropriated in faith by the Holy Spirit in the hearts of men; this is a continuous speech of God, His action and operation at all points, creating, correcting and extending the *Existenz* of man. "The Word *of* God"! This is a subjective genitive. This Word which is revelation, reconciliation, redemption, is *God's* action from first to last, an action which has man for its *object*. It is at no point something that man discovers for himself about God, man being, as it were, the subject and God the object. In all the divisions of dogmatics God is the Subject of the action, whatever aspect of this action be the topic of this or that particular section of the Church's considered language; whether election, or sanctification, doctrine of God, or doctrine of man, creation, redemption, first or last things. All things are done through the Word, and God is the Speaker of the operative Word. "Logically the questions are quite simply about the subject, predicate and

6 I.1.18.
7 II.1.61.

object of the short sentence, 'God speaks,' *Deus dixit*."
Barth tells us in the later editions of the first volume of his
Dogmatics that he stands by this formula "used somewhat
unguardedly and ambiguously" in the first edition.[8] The truth
seems to be that Barth's use here of "Subject" in the doctrine of "God's indissoluble subjectivity"[9] (i.e. *Subjektsein,*
"being Subject") combines the grammatical sense of "subject"—the word indicating the actor or active agent in the
typical sentence with transitive verb predicating action upon
the grammatical "object" as the thing acted upon—with the
technical use of "Subject" in epistemology, which indicates
the active pole of the Subject-Object relation of knowledge,
in which the Object is inert in the relation of being known.
There seems, at least, to be something like an oscillation
between the grammatical and the epistemological senses of
Subject and Object, or a leaning now upon the one, now
upon the other sense. One must be careful, therefore, not to
allow the popular, grammatical sense of Subject, extended
by Barth to mean God's originating, initiating, continuing
and ending activity in revelation, reconciliation and redemption, in all of which man is the Object of divine grace, not to
allow this sense to mislead us into thinking Barth means that
God is also the epistemological Subject in human knowledge
of God—a position to which some of his statements appear
to approximate; as, for example, in the second and third
sections of the second chapter of *The Doctrine of the Word
of God,* on God's revelation, where Jesus Christ as the becoming flesh of the Word is called "The objective reality
and possibility of revelation," and the outpouring of the
Holy Spirit "The subjective reality and possibility of revelation."[10] Barth is in no danger really of losing the distinction
between God and man here—were it otherwise he would
run the risk of saying that in man God knows Himself by
faith. "Man is the Subject of faith. It is not God but man
who believes":[11] this is Barth's explicit statement. And explicit statement could hardly go further than this: "God

[8] I.1.340.
[9] I.1.438.
[10] I.2.Inhalt VII.
[11] I.i.281.

steps over against the human Subject as Object in His Word, makes the human Subject capable of access to Himself, able to contemplate and comprehend (*anschauen und begreifen*) Himself as Object, through His Holy Spirit. But it is God in His relation to man and at the same time in His distinction from man with which real knowledge of God has to do. We thus distinguish our position from every sort of conception of the knowledge of God which is compelled to regard itself as the unity of being of man with God, according to which . . . the distinction of knower and known is left behind in knowledge."[12] But even here, where God offers Himself as Object to man's knowledge, He is, of course, still "indissolubly Subject," "the proper and primary active Subject of all real knowledge of God."[13] It is His own doing that He offers Himself in the event of Jesus Christ as Object; it is *Himself*, His own being and activity that He there offers; and, by a further operation of His own activity, man's *Exintenz* is enlarged and enabled to grasp what is there offered. God first and last; Father, Son and Holy Spirit; Creator, Reconciler, Redeemer; all is the mighty action and life of the one living and true God, in the speech which is and works salvation; and the Subject of this sentence "God speaks," co-extensive with this work of salvation, is God Himself, indissolubly Subject.

There belongs to Barth's doctrine of God as always Subject the further point that the God who offers Himself as the Object of saving knowledge reveals Himself in so doing as man's sovereign Lord, claiming obedience, manifesting the love in virtue of which He is to be feared, having known whom man can no longer desire the continuance of his own being without this precious enlargement of his existence. The Object rounds upon the human subject and asserts itself as Subject, as first in being and pre-eminence, as the author of human subjecthood, to whom is due submission and—as it turns out in the gospel, in the event of Jesus Christ—love. In the normal Subject-Object relation the Object is conceived as passive, at least in the relation of being known by the Subject. But the Object known in the religious encounter

12 II.1.9.
13 II.1.8.

of biblical faith is the living God, who reveals Himself as active in this relation, having made human Subjecthood in the beginning and now offering Himself as Object in this revelation, the concrete content of which, furthermore, is a claim or a call or a challenge to man's response. The knower knows that in this knowledge he was first of all known by Him whom he knows, through the grace of this revelation which is at the same time judgement. Once more the Object is Subject, the primary partner—but *revealed* as such, within and without disturbance to the epistemological Subject-Object relation, even where the revelation implies so much more. "Communion with Him who reveals Himself there," i.e. in the revelation attested to by the Bible, "means for man, in every case and under all circumstances, that He confronts him as a Thou confronts an I, and unites with him as a Thou unites with an I. All communion with this God is barred, of the kind . . . we might have with creatures, such that the Thou can be changed by the I into an It or a He, over which or whom the I thereby acquires powers of disposal . . . It cannot become an object."[14] This is to say that the *Thou* here known not only differs from mere objects or *It's* in the usual way in which encounter or intercourse with persons differs from apprehension of things (whether material objects or ideal objects of thought), but that the God of revelation is a unique *Thou*, establishing Himself in revelation as the Lord of man's life and of all things.

Two matters of perhaps unequal validity are hinted at in the language here used of this *Thou* who is supreme Subject, when it is said that this *Thou* cannot be changed into an *It* or a *He* "over which or whom the I thereby acquires powers of disposal." It is a fundamental interest of Barth that the God of the Bible cannot be argued to or known outside of the revelation in Jesus Christ. We need not dwell upon his repudiation of natural theology and general revelation, which have been sufficiently discussed elsewhere, but merely remind ourselves of these things here. They mean that man is held to be unable, out of his own knowledge gathered in the usual exercise of his faculties in science,

14 I.1.438.

philosophy, history, reflection on morals or aesthetics, to
arrive at the saving knowledge of God contained in the
biblical revelation of the living God as Creator, Reconciler,
Redeemer. He cannot *thus* know that *this* God *is,* or enter
into saving relation with Him. It is even doubtful if he can
come in this way to any certainty that *any* God exists, in
the manner in which the existence of God has been held to
matter to mankind. From this state of being without God
or hope in the world mankind has been delivered by the
coming of God into the world in the specific, particular,
historical revelation in Jesus Christ, prepared for, incarnate
in the fullness of the times, and now known in the Church
by the conviction which the Holy Spirit operates in the
hearts of believers on the basis of the Church's proclamation of her God-given message. There is absolutely no
guarantee of the truth of this message or the reality of this
experience of saving knowledge apart from the said conviction, which God Himself, who is the source and the content
of the message Himself, works in the believer to make him the
recipient of His salvation. God is every way Subject here:
He gives and man receives. Man takes and adjusts himself
to what is given and what is required: man is Object in this
relation, in this sense. Moreover, God never hands Himself
over or His salvation into man's hands to do what he likes
with. The relation is perpetuated in an ever-renewed taking
or receiving, in which God remains the Giver, remains Lord,
remains "indissolubly Subject." God is not objectified in His
gift in Jesus Christ, in the sense of becoming any dead thing
apart from His own life of continuous, renewed, repeated
encounter with man. Neither in the beginning nor in the
end, nor between the times, is He an object at man's disposal,
arrived at, enjoyed, trusted in, hoped in, by the exertion of
power from man's end of the relation. All is of God. And in
this indissoluble subjectivity of God (God's abiding *Subjektsein*
in all relations of His giving of Himself to men) is the only,
but also the supreme and unassailable and all-sufficient
guarantee of the complete objectivity of the Christian
revelation, the assurance of the faith which responds thereto.
Christian faith is not a probable hypothesis, nor even the

most probable hypothesis. It is the human end of a God-instituted and God-continued relation.

What is not quite so certain is the implication that in the ordinary course of knowledge the Object is usually at man's disposal, that knowledge of the world around and within him gained by the ordinary processes of scientific investigation and moral and aesthetic intuition (let the word pass for the meantime!) is a development of man's own being, a region of his own human *Existenz*. It is possible to suspect a vestigial survival of Barth's Kantianism here, of the Copernican revolution of the Critical Philosophy, which guaranteed absolute truth to certain kinds of knowledge by making things conform to the laws of man's mind, phenomena to the forms of sensuous perception in space and time and to the categories of the understanding. But even Kant knew that this did not mean that man made either himself or his world. The sensuous manifold is given, and behind the appearances are things-in-themselves. Control by the Object, as we have seen early in this course of lectures, is an admitted criterion of truth even in matters usually denominated "subjective": there is an opposition of truth versus falsehood even in art, in poetry, in painting. Whether this reflection opens up the possibility of a *rapprochement* between Barth's view of revelation and the rest of human knowledge is a matter into which we cannot go now. In the meanwhile we note that a certain degree of doubt of his epistemology, when he distinguishes between objects which are at man's disposal and the Object which is never at man's disposal, does not affect what he wants to say when he declares that God is never an Object in the sense of being at the disposal of human knowledge in its ordinary operations, or amenable to criteria of truth which take no account of the special, nay! the specific and unique nature of this Object, namely, that it is always, in Barth's sense of the word, Subject. We may agree with what he affirms, and yet be doubtful of what he denies, or of that with which he contrasts what he holds to be true.

It should by now be abundantly plain that Barth does say, and say repeatedly, that God appears to man as the Object of his knowledge. It should also begin to be plain both what is meant and what is disallowed by this manner of speaking, "that God gives Himself to be known by man in the revelation of His Word by means of the Holy Spirit means this: He comes before man as Subject in the relation of Object. In His revelation he is seen and understood of men (*angeschaut und begriffen*)."[15] On the very first page of the third volume of the *Dogmatik,* in the opening paragraphs of Chapter Five on "The Knowledge of God," we find, immediately following upon a statement of God's being the "grounding and realizing Subject of all that is here to be said and heard" that "all saying and hearing in the Church of Jesus Christ rests upon and is related to this, that God is known in the Church of Jesus Christ, i.e. that this Subject is objectively present (*gegenständlich gegenwärtig*) to him who speaks and hears; in the Church man really stands before God . . . the Object of his perception, his seeing, his understanding (*Wahrnehmung, Anchauen, Begreifen*)." This accumulation of terms from the technical language of the psychology and epistemology of the Subject-Object relation is impressive. But it must not blind us to the consideration that although "God appears upon the scene, enters the human circle of vision, just as other objects do" yet "God is not like any and every Object, not just an Object that gives itself to be known and is known like any other Object, not one that might awaken love, trust and obedience in the way that could be said of other Objects. His objectivity is the particular, the absolutely unique objectivity of God."[16] But, this being granted, "biblical faith lives by the objectivity of God."[17] Here it may be remarked that the index to any of the first three volumes of the *Dogmatik* abounds in references to "*Gott als Subjekt,*" while one will look in vain for a single entry under "*Gott als Objekt.*" Nevertheless there are numerous references to "*Gegenstand*" (Object) under "*Glaube*" (faith) in all three volumes, and two references under "*Gott*" to "*Gegenständlichkeit*" (objectivity) in the third volume, the most important in this connection. The choice of *Gegenstand* rather than *Objekt* is in itself significant. *Objekt* and *Objektivität* are terms at home in the epistemological context: *Objekt* is the

[15] II.1.8.
[16] II.1.13.
[17] *loc. cit.*

correlative of *Subjekt* in the *Subjekt-Objekt Verhältnis* (the Subject-Object relation); and *Objektivität* may mean either *Objektsein*, the state or condition of being an Object to a Subject in the knowledge relation, or it may mean actual existence in the "objective" world as contrasted with seeming existence, in the way of "subjective" fancy or illusion. It may also approximate to *Gegenständlichkeit*, the special kind of existence involved in being an object or thing, material or mental, real or imaginary. God, then, can be *Objekt* in the dispassionate, reflective, objective speech proper to theology, and the *Objectivität* of that truth, of the statements made about His being and works on the basis of faith is a matter of supreme concern to theology. But *Gegenstand* is the more appropriate term for the reality encountered in faith than *Objekt*; and it is unfortunate that we cannot distinguish between these two in English. Etymologically *Gegenstand* means that which stands over against something or somebody: *Objekt* is that which lies passive under the scrutiny of a *Subjekt* which finds it, discovers it, stumbles upon or over it. *Objekt* is suited to the knowledge relation, where the emphasis is upon the activity of the knowing *Subjekt*. *Gegenstand* is the better word for the present reality of God to man in encounter, where God has stepped down into the circle of man's sight, and stands over against him as commanding correlative, as *Du* and not *Es* (*Thou* and not *It*), as the initiating, controlling Subject who is never at man's disposal, but who calls for man's obedience to God's control which is love and therefore to be feared in the possibility of its loss.

God, we have heard, is not any and every kind of Object. He is not *a* particular Object, although He particularizes Himself in special revelation through a peculiar people with whom He enters into special relations of nearness in a covenant, and through whose history He prepares for the supreme event in revelation, the taking flesh of the Word of God in Jesus Christ, continued in the work of the Holy Spirit in the Church. God is not a particular object present to men's senses. Barth agrees with Kierkegaard that "the immediate relationship to God is paganism."[18] God is for us

18 *Postscript*, p. 218.

mediately objective (*mittelbar gegenständlich*); not direct, but indirect, not unclothed but clothed upon, under signs and under coverings of *other* objects different from Himself."[19] God is immediately objective only to Himself: He is "objective to Himself" and He is "immediate to Himself" in "primary objectivity" in the life of the Trinity.[20] "For the Father is without middle term Object (*Gegenstand*) to the Son, the Son to the Father."[21] The objectivity of God to us in His revelation is *secondary,* mediated through objects that we can see, hear or handle, through objects appropriate to our comprehension, but which are distinguished from God Himself in His immediacy. To this extent and in this sense revelation is at one and the same time an unveiling and a veiling of God, whose face no man can see and live. That God chooses the objects that are to reveal Him, and such objects as can and do reveal Him, that He Himself sets going and carries through this revelation, that He gives power to man in the Holy Spirit to recognize His signs as revelation of Himself; all these operations of God as Subject in revelation guarantee that it is God Himself who is thereby revealed, the true God, though veiled under husks and coverings. And the possibility of the one objectivity is laid up in the other, the secondary in the primary. God can be known as Object by man because He is Object to Himself; the importation of the Subject-Object relation is no distortion foreign to His essential being, His very nature comes over in the process, although in limitation appropriate to our creaturely condition.

Through man's relation to God's inherent *Gegenständlichkeit* is an indirect one in revelation, yet his relation to the *Gegenstände,* the objects which reveal God, is altogether direct; these are part of the objective reality which constitutes man's environment.[22] "He stands directly before an other Object, one Object from among other Objects. The objectivity of this other Object stands for (*tritt ein für*) the objectivity of God. In the objectivity of this other Object he

[19] II.1.16.
[20] II.1.16, 15.
[21] II.1.16.
[22] II.1.17, top page.

knows God. . . . This other Object he sees, perceives, cognizes." Once again the technicalities of the psychology of perception (*Anschauung, Wahrnehmung, Begreifen*). "But in and with this other Object the objectivity of God. This other Object is thus the medium through which God gives Himself to be known by him and in which man knows God."[23] This capacity of creaturely reality to convey knowledge of God, to act as *sign,* is, as the word "sign" itself and the prepositions "in and with" suggest, with their reminders of the historic vocabulary of the Lutheran doctrine of the Lord's Supper, properly described as *sacramental.* "Revelation means the *giving of signs* . . . means sacrament, i.e. the self-attestation of God, the manifestation of His truth and therewith also of the truth in which He knows Himself, in the form of creaturely objectivity and thus in the form and measure appropriate to our creaturely understanding."[24] But that God is thus known through works of His creating does not mean that this sacramental quality inheres in nature as such, either as a whole or in its parts. It is no generalized mystical meaning universally accessible to "the spiritual eye" of enlightened natural man.

> "Earth's crammed with heaven,
> And every common bush afire with God,
> But only he who sees takes off his shoes."

Barth would not allow that Mrs. Browning gives here a correct Midrash upon "the place of the bush" in the Exodus story. This would be one more denial of the subjectivity of God in revelation; one more denial that man's place in the knowledge of God is a *Nachher,* a coming after God always, a subordination as recipient and not discoverer of God's truth; one more denial that his standing here is the *status gratiae.*[25] The sacramental quality of creation is possibility only; a possibility laid into it doubtless from the beginning when all things were made by the Word of God, and made for the appearing of the Word in the fullness of the times in

[23] II.1.16.
[24] II.1.56.
[25] II.1.21.

the flesh or human nature of Jesus Christ. It is from this
event, the incarnation, the taking to Himself flesh by the
eternal Son of God and being found in fashion as a man,
that the sacramental quality and capacity of creaturely
reality is to be interpreted. "*Gratia unionis*, i.e. on the basis
of and through its being united with the eternal Word of God
this creature (the human nature of Jesus Christ) becomes the
work and sign of God par excellence (*hervorgehobenen und
ausgezeichnetes*). In the light of this, that the eternal Word
itself became flesh; in the light of this, that revelation of
God has happened once for all in Jesus Christ, we recognize
the identical revelation of God in every quarter where witness
to this event is borne in expectation and recollection; in the
light of *this:* looking at the witness to God everywhere that
there is witness to this happening . . . a sacramental continuity
backwards in the existence of the nation of Israel, whose
Messiah He is, and forwards in the existence of the Aposto-
late and the Church founded on the work of the Apostles."[26]
Whatever may be the truth of a cosmic Christ, it is a truth
to be read in terms of the specific revelation of God concentrated in a particular thread of historical happening. This
objectivity of God must always constitute an *offence* to the
generalizing intellect which equates truth with the discovery
of universals. God and His truth are not universals—not
even, in the language of idealism, concrete universals. Although He is not *an* Object, yet there is only the *one* living and
true God. He is completely Individual, unique even in His
universality and the distinctions within His personal being,
the initiator of particularist action in revelation so specific
as to hide Him from those who cannot read His signs, see
through the secondary to the primary objectivity of the
Objects which He causes to reveal Him.

With this problem, that of the indirectness, the veiled
character of God's revelation, of a particularity in its
objectivity which can actually conceal its character of revelation, we are brought in sight of the last range of topics to
be discussed in this connection; the problems, namely, con-
nected with the knowledge of God as "faith-knowledge"
(*Glaubenserkenntnis*), as a revelation "from faith to faith."

[26] II.1.58.

How is it that revelation sometimes fails to reveal God, that His signs sometimes fail to signify? Is not the fact that we have to fall back here upon talk of "faith" at all a final confession of "subjectivity"? That the objectivity with which revelation occupies itself fails in the end to be objective enough, comes short of that objectivity or assurance of truth and reality, of which we have experience (or conceive that we have experience) in other departments of life and thought? Does not all talk of "the obedience of faith" imply that here the objectivity of revelation depends after all upon an existentialist decision which *we* make (or do not make), so that this truth becomes true for us because we choose to have it so?

We have seen that the Objects through which revelation is made are, according to Barth, "objective" enough; they are "really there," parts of environmental reality which can be seen, perceived, laid hold upon by mental processes. God meets us in actual historical events, in living men and women, in the thoughts and actions of the revealing personalities in salvation-history, all in their actuality and in the record of these things, written, proclaimed, preached. What may fail to appear "objective" is the signification of these Objects said to attach to them by the witness of the Christian Church. Their objectivity does not become a sign of God's objectivity, in and through them. Why, or, how not? Partly, of course, that God is veiled in them, as well as revealed, even to the most confident and assured faith. It is granted that this objectivity is secondary in respect of the primary objectivity of God himself, that they are not in themselves God, that they remain creatures and retain their creaturely nature even in revelation.[27] If God remains mystery even to the obedience of faith there is, then, no marvel if He is not recognized by unfaith. But this is hardly the real reason why the signs do not signify. The veiling remains, the mystery of God's being and the marvel of His grace are truly known as such only to faith. It is precisely the believer who "loves to lose himself in a mystery, to pursue his reason to an *O*

---

[27] *Ohne dass es aufhörte, diese vestimmte geschöpfliche Wirklichkeit zu sein, also ohne dass es an sich mit Gott identisch würde.* II.1.17, top page.

altitudo." Neither is it because the signs are not sufficiently compelling to arrest and force faith. This is a wrong conception of faith altogether, which is no compelled obedience. *Sign* is used by Barth, it would appear, as much on the basis of its technical use in Reformation doctrine of the sacraments as on the Johannine use of *semeion* to express the revelatory quality of Jesus' mighty (and usually marvellous) works. Kierkegaard had written: "If God, for example, had taken on the figure of a very rare and tremendously large green bird, with a red beak, sitting on a tree on a mound, and perhaps whistling in an unheard of manner—then . . . man would have been able to get his eyes open . . . All paganism consists in this, that God is related to man directly, as the obviously extraordinary to the astonished observer. But the spiritual relationship to God in the truth . . . corresponds to the divine elusiveness that God has absolutely nothing obvious about Him."[28] This "green bird" would be a *sign* in the sense in which the Synoptic Gospels consistently represent Jesus refusing the demand for a sign. And this is not the sense in which Barth bases revelation upon "signs." It is noteworthy that he does not appear to regard the resurrection of Jesus as a sign of this sort. "Even they (*sc.* the Apostles) stood before a veil (*Hülle*), before a sign, before a work of God: in the manger at Bethlehem and on the cross at Golgotha there took place that indeed in which God gave Himself to be known to them. That, in the light of the resurrection and in the course of the 'forty days,' they saw that for what it really is, as God's own presence and action, makes no difference to the fact that what they saw, even during the forty days, was *this:* indubitable secondary objectivity and precisely in this as such, witnessed to thereby, primary objectivity and thus they knew God Himself."[29] This passage is not without ambiguity; but it appears to rank the resurrection as part of the events of the forty days, and to hold that, although the appearances of Jesus to His disciples after His death cast light retrospectively upon His birth and death as divine dealing with and for men, yet these appearances, and the resurrection itself as the beginning of the

[28] *Postscript*, p. 219.
[29] II.1.20.

series, cannot be appealed to after the fashion of paganism as direct, immediate, objective presence of God in a theophany confounding all possible doubt. Barth then would refuse the apologetic which sets out from the resurrection as "the most certain event in history," and seeks to present Christianity as having "objective" historical certification. The gospel repudiates objective compulsion of this sort—even were its historical origins completely certified. No! the root reason why for some the signs of biblical revelation do not signify God's presence and mighty acts for our salvation is not so much that the Jewish demand for a sign is refused, but that the Greek seeking after wisdom, a wisdom based upon purely human premises and processes, is offended by the kind of objectivity the gospel proclaims. "Precisely in face of God's works and signs what happens is *offence*, which rejects the presumption that would recognize the objectivity of God in the objectivity of the creature, rejects this because of the too great humiliation and estrangement of God's glory in these objects of belief and recognition, and therewith rejects God Himself, God in the grace of His condescension to the creature."[30]

With this, some account of the Barthian explanation is given of why signs of God's presence and activity fail to signify to unbelief. One kind of Object God cannot, in the nature of the case, be, except to Himself. A faith which demands this sort of Object is bound to be disappointed. And the kind of Object in which faith does see and know God present has its own creaturely objectivity beyond which unbelief cannot see. When we come to ask why faith believes, however, we come up against an ultimate problem which has its analogies in the process whereby conviction or persuasion is produced in any matter involving more than the mere intelligence, but affecting man's being as a whole, conscience, moral nature, action and feeling—in short, his *Existenz*—but a problem which has its peculiar difficulties in that here is involved the final mystery of God's grace and man's own will. Faith is knowledge, but it is the knowledge of faith: the circle is inescapable. "God gives Himself to be known in His will directed towards us; God is known when

[30] II.1.60.

we submit ourselves—or put ourselves at the disposal of (*indem wir . . . fügsam werden*) this His will; this circular movement (*Kreislauf*) obviously corresponds exactly to what in the Old and New Testaments is called knowledge of God."[31] But a circle need not be a vicious circle! In many departments of life we are shut up to conviction of this sort. It is no fatal argument against faith that its movement is circular, that its knowledge is gained from the standpoint of itself—so long as it is knowledge related to its Object, and is not subjectivity chasing its own tail! "In faith there happens something which happens everywhere and always in the same way when man enters into that relation of being bound to and differentiated from an Object, when his subjectivity is opened up for an objectivity and thereby is grounded and determined anew. In faith this occurs in an altogether different fashion. Its peculiarity consists in the peculiarity, in the unique character of its Object, God."[32] If this experience produces its own conviction, if its truth is seen in its own light, if it is existential truth found in existential encounter, in which Subject and Object mutually interpenetrate and affect each other, opening up new ranges of insight and activity, as contrasted with the more purely "objective" truth which belongs to science, where the nature of the Object is comparatively unmodified by the Subject (so we suppose!) and the Subject is comparatively indifferent to the Object; if all this is so, is the validity of the knowledge so gained impugned as to its own kind of truth by being "inside knowledge"? Is the knowledge of two people in love with one another less true than the careless world's knowledge of the principals?

"The totality of the positive relation of man to God who gives Himself to be known in His Word, the event of turning towards, opening oneself up to, the yielding of man to this God, the Yes! which he himself speaks in his 'heart' over against this God, as he knows himself bound, as altogether under obligation, the engagement of himself in which before God he recognizes himself as belonging to God and so declares himself in the light of the clear conviction that God is

[31] II.1.30.
[32] II.1.14.

God and *his* God—that is faith. And one must immediately add this: Faith, as the positive relation of man to God comes from God Himself in so far as it is first and last grounded in this, namely, that God meets man in this turning towards Him on man's part, in this Yes! in this engagement called forth by His Word, has therefore become Object to man, that in this objectivity of His has gifted to man through the Holy Spirit the light of the conviction that He is God and his God, and that therefore He has called forth this Yes! this engagement on man's part."[33] All the elements of Barth's view of faith come into view in this paragraph: it merely remains for us to bring them into clear and distinct view. We may as well admit that such a position disposes of many difficulties arising from the intellectualist bedevilment of the concept of faith, and sets it clearly in the context of existential encounter and response. There is decision and choice in faith, certainly; but we do not decide for or against faith from the outside, from a standpoint of superior certainty otherwise derived—nor yet out of the despair of complete uncertainty! Faith is response to a revelation of One who shows Himself Lord and our Lord; in the light and in the power of that self-authenticating witness we yield our obedience to a claim we see binding us. Obedience is the obedience of faith: decision is decision in faith: venture is adventure in faith.[34] It is not the "venture of faith": it is not the "will to believe." When we engage ourselves it is not to the most probable or the most noble hypothesis. This is all on the human level, something man does, and not God. The obedience of faith in Barth is neither caprice,[35] although it *is* choice in freedom, nor is it willed suspension of doubt to end despair.[36] It is neither *salto mortale* nor *sacrificium intellectus,* for its Object is not an intellectual proposition or theory which we have devised and find ourselves in despair of ever or sufficiently proving. All these positions spring from too intellectualistic an idea of the Object, which is here the Word of God in the event of Jesus Christ, the

[33] II.1.11.
[34] I.1.529.
[35] *Wilkur;* see, II.1.6.
[36] *loc. cit.*

coming of the Word made flesh. And although the New Testament message is often formulated "Jesus is the Christ," the Object of faith is not doctrinal propositions about Jesus, but the divine presence or objectivity encountered in Him. Parenthetically we may remark that faith will not, on such a view as Barth's, sanction the willed decision of purely historical matter regarding Him, the cutting of Gordian knots as to whether He was or was not "born of a Virgin" or "rose again the third day." Faith will dispose to a different evaluation of the historical evidence on such matters; it cannot arise from a purely historical positive finding with regard to them. All these positions presuppose that man is in a position to judge the Word of God; whereas in biblical revelation it is the Word which judges man. The Word, on such a view as Barth's, either enables unto faith, or condemns unto the disobedience of sin. This is, of course, a view which is only possible from the standpoint of faith itself, but surely one which faith is, from its own standpoint, entitled to make. Once again we are reminded of the "theological circle." It is doubtful whether, with Barth, we must therefore dismiss all apologetic considerations as irrelevant.

What then of acceptance, of commitment to the Object which reveals its right to be acknowledged Subject, sovereign Lord of life? All this talk of will, choice, decision, commitment, obedience (even if "obedience of faith"), all these terms surely imply that there is something that man must do for and of himself with regard to this Object which confronts him with the necessity, the imperative of choice. Why else this talk of sin in this connection? Barth has not finally removed all perplexities here. But his representations on the relations of the human and the divine subjectivity in this encounter constitute a profound and subtle account of a crucial problem for religion, and perhaps for more than religion. Of course, man acts in faith; in the original decision by which he responds to the claim made upon him by God in His revelation of Himself as Lord, and in the continued acting by which he keeps himself in faith. There is a moving exegesis (if not a very obvious one!) in this connection of a petition in the Lord's Prayer. "Lead us not into temptation —the temptation of an objectivistic, uncommunicated con-

ception of God's objectivity, not arising from obedience."[37]
This is the context in which alone Barth discusses man's
action in faith. It is an action and a freedom wholly determined and enabled by God's prior action in revelation, such
that even here God remains Subject. "Man *acts* by believing,
but the fact that he *believes* by acting is *God's* act. Man is
the subject of faith. It is not God but man who believes. But
the very fact of a man thus being subject in faith is bracketed
as the predicate of the subject, *God,* bracketed exactly as the
Creator embraces His creature, the merciful God sinful man,
i.e. so that there is no departure from man's being a subject,
and this very thing, the ego of man as such, is still only
derivable from the Thou of the Subject, God."[38] This position
is formally defined in the statement that "the Holy Spirit is
the subjective reality of revelation."[39] This does *not* mean
that "God gives the condition of faith" in the form of a
psychological disposition or a rearrangement of the human
consciousness, any more than it means that there is some sort
of displacement of the human Subject by the divine Subject, of man's ego by the Third Person in the Trinity, nor
yet by any "confusion or intermingling" of these Subjects.
Faith is not a psychological freak. The "condition" which is
given by God, upon which faith supervenes, is the reality of
revelation, objective reality in the total event of Jesus Christ.
We must beware of speaking as if it were the Holy Spirit that
acts when God's call in revelation is obeyed, and man
only acts when that call is disregarded and its claim disallowed. "The statements about the operation of the Holy
Spirit are statements the Subject of which is God and not
man, and under no circumstances could they be translated
into statements about men. They speak of the relation of God
to man, to his knowledge, will and feeling, to his experience
active and passive, to his heart and conscience, to his soul-
and-body existence, but they cannot be reversed and regarded
as statements about the existence of man. To say that
God the Holy Spirit is the Redeemer who makes us free
is a statement of knowledge and praise of God. We are

[37] II.1.27.
[38] I.1.281.
[39] I.11.222.

ourselves in virtue of this statement, redeemed, set free, children of God in faith, in the faith which we confess by this statement; but it means, in the act of God if which this statement speaks. This existence of ours is enclosed within the act of God."[40] If these statements of Barth appear to endanger they can also be read as presupposing a natural freedom of man, the fundamental feature of his creaturely subjectivity. But the only freedom which is in question in Christian dogmatics is the freedom which is enclosed within the act of God in revelation which is salvation. And the thing most relevant and alone worth saying in this connection is that this formal possibility of man's *Existenz* is realized within the Christian revelation in an actuality of content which is inconceivable apart from that revelation. The formal possibility is nothing in comparison with the freedom and life of the children of God, where man has been lifted into a sphere where his decision is not the decisive matter, but the very possibility of his deciding for it has been made possible by God's grace in the showing of His salvation.

The rejection on all mechanistic views of the operation of the Holy Spirit, the confirmation of man's distinction from God in the intercourse of encounter, where the statements that are significant are, as we have just seen, statements of which God is the Subject and not man, all this is implied in the words "called forth" which Barth uses of the human response to revelation. *Hervorgerufen* is the negation of all compelled, causally produced or determined assent to revelation in the obedience of faith. "Knowledge of God comes to pass in *obedience* towards God—not in a slavish but a childlike obedience, not in a blind but a seeing obedience, not in a compelled but a free obedience—and precisely so, in a real obedience . . . But this obedience itself is not only called forth (*hervorgerufen*) through (its) Object, but also determined and characterized thereby; it can be none other than this childlike seeing, free obedience, which flows from the fear of God, and is rooted in the love of God."[41]

[40] I.1.529.
[41] II.1.39.

It may be asked, of course, how anything can be *called forth* which is not in some sense already there! Is there not something here which is surely man's own in distinction from what is God's doing, all question apart of what God does in creating man in the beginning? Is there not something here which is of the same kind as the appeal to conscience, to moral or religious sense, to the awareness of creaturely dependence—to something which belongs to human *Existenz* in general and as such? It would be the height of unwisdom in these closing pages to raise again the debate regarding the *Anknüpfungspunkt*, the point of connection between revelation and that in man to which revelation makes its appeal. Without even expressing any opinion on the merits of the famous controversy we may remind ourselves of some of Barth's statements in the *Dogmatics*. The man who decides in faith is not what he would be apart from what revelation makes him in proposing itself for his decision. Revelation extends his *Existenz* by a dimension which was not there before. "In faith he (*sc.* the believer) must regard . . . his very self in its activity . . . as determined by the Word of God . . . as someone else whom he had no capacity to become, whom he has also no power to be, whom, therefore, he is not free to become or to be . . . in short, whom he *can* only be by being him."[42] Certainly man is capable of fear and of love, just as he is capable of seeing and comprehending objects presented to his perception generally. But he is not capable of fearing and loving the living God of revelation until this God has presented Himself to his seeing and comprehending, as One whom he may *dare*[43] take it upon him to fear and love (and fear because he loves) in an Object which, while it presents itself to his senses in the historic event of Jesus Christ, is yet different from all other Objects of his perception in that this is the indirect objectivity of God Himself. This new fear and love and perception are works of which God is the author, predicates of which He is the Subject, and the conviction of their truth and reality are the doing of the Holy Spirit in the heart of man, subjectively appropriating the objective truth in Jesus Christ.

[42] I.1.280f.
[43] *dürfen;* see II.1.40f.

There is nothing here that is man's own prior possession, unless possibility itself is to be reckoned a possession. Is *posse* an *esse*, and is it *man's possession?* Man is addressable (*redbar*). A "point of contact," an *Anknüpfungspunkt* between revelation and response, will submit to the general definition of a point as "that which has position but no magnitude." What does this imply as to *Existenz?* In a sense, according to Karl Barth, we are more certain of God's *Existenz* than of our own, both *that* He is and *what* He is. In faith we start out from Him, and from His revelation we learn what we are and what we may become through His Word. "Our redemption is not a relation such as we can review, i.e. such as we can understand both ways, from God's side and from our own. Paradoxically enough we can only understand it from God's side."[44] Faith understands human *Existenz* from God's side, although not as a completed magnitude. This, of course, refers to redeemed *Existenz,* the medium of which is faith. But the understanding may be presumed to extend backwards to human *Existenz* generally, as that which by the marvel of God's grace (which we have come to know) *can* be redeemed, which contains an un-dreamt of *posse* that here stands revealed.

Last word of all. Barth's doctrine of the Holy Spirit as the subjective reality of revelation, of God as Subject in His Word creating the new *Existenz* of redeemed human nature, the subjective reality of believing obedience, in fear and trembling lest it lose the love which has first loved us; this doctrine which nevertheless refuses to lose man in God, but to the end insists upon the distinction of persons in the encounter of Subjects, the divine and the human; this doctrine can be regarded as the supreme example of the existential process which Martin Buber describes in the formula *Ich werde am Du.* In deference to the indissoluble, irremovable subjectivity of God, to man's coming always *after* God, his action being essentially response, our love being because He first loved, the formula might be more Christianly transposed to read *Am Du Ich werde.* Barth has always insisted against his critics that his position is *also* a humanism. It is not the denial or the denigration of man. Man finds his true and only last-

44 I.1.529.

ing dignity as the child of God. "There is no departure from man's being a subject" involved in the prior position that "this very thing, the ego of man as such, is still only derivable from the Thou of the Subject, God."[45] Faith, by which the Christian lives, is *hervorgerufen*, not *verursacht*, called forth and not causally created. And in the progress from faith to faith, set forth in the section of the *Dogmatik* with which we have been principally concerned, that on the "Knowledge of God" (II 1.1-67), we can trace by anticipation the operation of the same principle in sanctification and glorification. The New Testament statement of the Buberian and Barthian doctrine of *Ich werde am Du* runs thus: "We all, with open face beholding as in a glass the glory of the Lord, are changed into the same image from glory to glory, even as by the Spirit of the Lord."[46] And the final hope of the Christian envisages the continued operation of the same principle: "Beloved, now are we the sons of God, and it doth not yet appear what we shall be: but we know that, when he shall appear, we shall be like him; for we shall see him as he is."[47]

[45] I.1.281.
[46] II Cor. 3.18.
[47] I John 3.2.

Chapter 7

Summary And Conclusions

WE HAVE COME to the end of our series of studies on the place of the Subject-Object relation and the antithesis of subjective and objective in some representative and influential theological thinking of the last hundred years. Can we offer any definite results or conclusions of the course as a whole? Does any sort of lesson or moral, positive or negative, emerge for theological construction in our own time?

At the very least we have thrown light upon a wide variety of terminological usage, and are in a position to reinforce the well-known warning against the supposition that words, even technical terms in philosophy or theology, must always mean the same thing for different thinkers and writers. We began by pointing out that the terminology of Subject and Object in its modern usage derives from the Kantian epistemology. But how little light, for example, does the Kantian use of these terms throw upon the theological catchword studied in the last chapter, "The Subject which is never Object," as applied to God! Kant could have agreed that God can never be the Object of sensuous perception to a human subject, or even that God cannot be a finite particular existent or occurrence in the world in space and time. He might even have pointed out that no Subject is ever Object to itself or others, in the strictly epistemological sense. The Subject, when it is not a *noumenal* reality, is at most a logical presupposition, and neither of these can come before mind as a sensuous Object. But how far removed are either of these positions from the wealth of meaning the formula can be made to hold on the basis of the Barthian doctrine of God's ineluctable subjecthood! A whole theology of God's sovereignty and initiative in creation, revelation and redemption is implicit in Barth's use of the term Subject as applied to God; and similarly, his use of Object recalls an elaborate doctrine of man's subordination and dependence, the obedience of faith in the *status gratiae,* in the appropriation of salvation. Moreover, the Kantian usage actually stands in the way of Barth's subtle elaboration of how God does become Object to the faith-knowledge of the human Subject, in the Christian revelation; a becoming Object in matters open to sensuous perception, though not simply identical with these; a divine objectivity to man's perception which is yet "bracketed within" the all-embracing indefeasible subjectivity of God.

So too, having touched on the term subjectivity, we must note that the subjectivity which is truth, according to Kierkegaard, cannot be understood by reference to any Kantian use of the word. In Kierkegaard subjectivity is a characteristically defined exercise of human thought and will in face of a particular, indeed, a unique Object; a blend of activity and passivity evoked in believing hearts and lives by the entrance of the Eternal into history as an individual Man; a concrete conception of spirituality, in short, far advanced in content upon the Kantian Subject of necessary knowledge in its activity in an empirical ego.

Terms, we realize once again, and with renewed emphasis, must be taken in their context. The particular usage of each philosopher and theologian must be attended to for the precise shade of meaning he attaches to the traditional technicalities of his study. The terms Subject and Object, and their derivatives, are no exception to this rule. Terminology cannot stand still, for reason itself has a history. The conceptual apparatus with which thought tackles its problems is not an identical corpus in all times and places. Mind grows gradually aware of the structure of the thought-forms which prove adequate to the reality it seeks to articulate and so understand. Reason may be the same process in all its manifestations, yet its formulas be in course of continual modification, adjustment, definition. The Idea itself may be a pattern laid up eternal in the heavens. Meanwhile man is on earth; and the heavenly pattern must not be prematurely identified with the "Table of the Categories" in the *Critique of Pure Reason.*

Turning from terminology to the substance of the matters studied, the course as a whole might be described as exhibiting a progressive concretion of the Subject and an increasing emphasis upon the contribution of the Subject to knowledge of the Object, in certain departments of thought. We have to recognize, it may be with some disappointment, that no particular ontology is deducible from the bare form of knowledge in the Subject-Object relation. This is a logical abstraction, and any particular metaphysics associated with epistemology is presupposed by it, rather than inferred from it. It is part of our situation that we are inevitably and inescapably *inside* the knowledge relation, from the start and to the end, and so cannot step outside of ourselves to an indifferent standpoint from which to view and adjust the relations of thought and being. Thought and being are together from the beginning. All discrimination of the contribution of the one side of the relation to the other is an analysis of a concrete togetherness of thought and being in a particular department of existence. Since, moreover, all possible Objects of thought come before mind in a relation of Subject and Object— the wildest chimeras, the grossest illusions, as well as the soberest "matters of fact"—any discussion of the contribution of Subject to Object, of Object to Subject, of the proportions of subjectivity to objectivity in a particular topic, must have in view some particular sphere of actual concrete existence in which the Subject is more than the logical presupposition of knowledge in general, and the Object is viewed in relation to some actual concrete interest or preoccupation on the part of the Subject. Does the preoccupation of the Subject with the Object here in any way modify the nature of the Object? If it is here known in a different way, does that modification extend to the Object in itself, or only to the Object in this particular relation to the Subject? If this last, what becomes of the *objectivity* of the knowledge so gained? Granted that it is not the objectivity of natural science, granted that is the objectivity of morals or aesthetics or religion or whatever is in question, what becomes of that "control by the Object" which seems inseparable from the criterion of truth?

The Kantian reduction of the Subject to the pin-point of existence necessary to support the synthetic activity revealed in the organization of sense into perception and understanding, left the formal conditions of necessary knowledge with the Subject but threw all concrete knowledge of the nature of things on to the side of the Object presented. Kant himself was aware that the actually existing Subject is more than an epistemological presupposition: it exists as an empirical ego, a self or *psyche*—whose doings are immediately annexed by the natural science of psychology and studied in terms of natural necessity. Only in moral experience does he find himself compelled to admit the existence of the self as will and free. But this really existing, active and free concrete Subject cannot contribute anything to the knowledge of the Objects presented to it, in proper sense of the word "knowledge."

In Kierkegaard it is claimed that this position cannot be finally retained; although Kierkegaard finds himself closer to Kant than to Hegel in whom German idealism closes. Necessary knowledge has argued away actuality and existence. It must matter to the Subject—even the Subject of necessary knowledge—that it exists, that it is more than the formal possibility and presupposition of necessary knowledge. The living, existing self cannot lose itself in the objective world of knowledge, natural or philosophical. All knowledge *is* for a living, existing knower, a Subject immersed in the element of time and "becoming," dealing with Objects which in their turn are actual existences or happenings. The Subject of knowledge is a concrete experiencing existence or existent, and contrariwise knowledge is a particular, limited function of an existing, experiencing Subject or self. This concrete self, moreover, as spirit (for Kierkegaard is in debt to Hegel as well as in revolt against his misunderstandings and excesses) is the self-realization of its own *posse* as *esse*, is self-transcending ideality, exists for itself as an idea of itself going beyond its actual existence and ever calling for translation by itself into itself. In the moral aspect of this process (for the process has its natural aspect as the existence of a being immersed in time and becoming) spirit is forbidden to lose this quality of itself in indifferent objectivity. In religious experience it is all inwardness, independence of the outward or rather of the merely outward, appropriation of the objective elements of tradition and community, translation of the external circumstances of life into its own substance, as attitude, mood, pathos. In Christianity it is a highly particular form of such inwardness deriving from encounter with a unique historical event, the entrance into time and history of the Eternal in an individual Man. This reverses the categories of human thought and life in all other immanent activites, and is appropriated in face of the objective appearances of things in all other departments of experience, in a supreme passion of subjectivity which is called faith.

Whatever may be thought of this account of Christianity it is at all events an evaluation of the objective appearance of things in terms of a highly subjective activity: truth cannot be known apart from the relation of things to a Subject, to one particular form of spirituality. Such is the claim of the Christian religion and faith. It is not said that the Subject here creates it Object—far from it. The Object here is such as no Subject ever could create. It is set forth as having happened apart from all previous conception of the possibility of its happening: the incredible, the inconceivable, is reported as having actually happened, at a definite point in time and place. But a world of supremely important objective reality is here disclosed to a particular activity of the human Subject, apart from which the Object is not known as such. Truth here does not lie on the side of an unappropriated, unmediated Object. In a particular department of knowledge and truth —a department for which determinative influence upon all truth else is claimed—we meet with an Object which is not definable, whether as to its existence as Object or as to its quality and significance, apart from the Subject's implication in the Object and attitude towards it.

This view of the Subject as existence and self-realizing ideality is carried on in the philosophy of Martin Heidegger, with an emphasis on the Subject's contribution to the Object of the most radical character. Not only in the sphere of religious faith or in morals but in that of general phenomenology, the philosophical description of the basic structures of existences, as well as in the realm of natural science itself, things are to be defined in terms of the Subject's relation to them, attitude towards them, concern with them. A hammer as tool is obviously an existent related to human purpose, and actually *is* such a tool when it is being used (*Zuhandenheit*). As an object in space and time it is present to human perception (*Vorhandenheit*), and even as an object with weight and other qualities it is so defined in relation to the "project" of natural science, a human preoccupation and concern. Nowhere do we escape the reference to the Subject on the level of objective speech, in the ontological quest for reality. The Subject in its turn, however, is opened up to its Objects in its very innermost being. *Dasein*, the kind of existence appropriate to human beings, is being-with the *Umwelt* of things and the *Mitwelt* of persons; it is *Sorge*, concern with other existences, animate and inanimate. This is an interpenetration of the Subject by its Objects, equally real with that of Objects by the Subject. Subject, further, is insubstantial being, a kind of 'nothingness' suspended between the two total 'nothingnesses' of the human being's non-existence before birth and his cessation of existence at death. Yet the meaning of existence is read off in terms of the Subject, the human centre or point of relation, the kind of being in which being and reason meet and so provide the only key in our hands to an ontology. Mutual implication and interpenetration cannot be carried further in the case of Subject and Object; although here the 'concretion' of the Subject might also be described as its complete and total evisceration. A second instalment of Heidegger's enterprise promises a fundamental 'Meaning of Being' (*Sinn von Sein*) in terms of the preliminary inquiry into the nature of *Dasein*, the structure of human existence. It will still be a *meaning*, a construct of existence for mind. Objectivity apart from subjectivity for ever escapes us in the quest for ultimate truth. Once again there is a victory for the Subject.

In Martin Buber the emphasis upon creative subjectivity is equally evident. According to the existential word which man speaks, his environment passes from mere factual objectivity to living relation and dialogue with the cosmos. There is apparent depreciation of the logical and epistemological Subject as only capable of a knowledge which scratches at the surface of things. But the concrete Subject, the living self, the existing I, emerges as all the more central and determinative in its power to go forth to meet the challenge of the world of nature and its fellow-men, the invitation to enter upon real life in relation, to speak *Thou* to these emanations of an eternal *Thou-ness* by which the *I* is addressed. The roots of morality and communal life, as well as of the intellectual life, art, poetry, are to be found in such meeting with the Other in a wholeness of experience which is the substance of religion. The only doubt which remained with us here was whether the Subject, in this exercise of the power of entering into relation, might not be conceived as virtually creating this aspect of the universe as *Thou*. Buber certainly intends a real revelation of itself as *Thou* by man's world, a sustaining, embracing quality of *Thou-ness* in things, calling forth man's recognition of itself. This goes beyond Heidegger. The concrete Subject (only Buber is not fond of this word) is here the bearer not just of knowledge, scientific or philosophical, but also of "the life of relation," social life, artistic creation, religious experience (although, once again, Buber repudiates the word). Heidegger professes to practise pure phenomenology, apart from ethical concern, in an objectivity untinctured by any flavour of "value."

Finally, in the specifically Christian theology of Karl Barth, though the Subject of which we hear most is the divine Subject or God, and man's status is always that of a *Nachher*, the secondary and subordinate standing of the *status gratiae*, in which he is Object rather than Subject, the dogmatic work issues in a definition of the human Subject in relation to the divine Object of saving knowledge, a definition of extraordinary subtlety in its particularity and concreteness. Truth here is for a faith-knowledge not available or attainable outside a condition and disposition of the entire human Subject, in obedience, trust and response to a unique and specific revelation. Both Subject and Object here are entirely concrete and particular; both are defined in their existence and content by a unique divine activity, the Christian revelation of salvation.

The development we have thus traced in the gradual concretion of the Kantian epistemological Subject has received its terminology from Kierkegaard. It is the addition of existence to idea. The existentialist modification of the Subject proceeds at two levels: (*a*) The Subject is actual factual concrete existence in real space and time—we might say, in geographical space and historical time. Besides psychology, anthropology, morality, religion, besides these fresh generalizations of the concrete, there enter into any living, acting, experiencing Subject as self the particularities of historical happening and individual experience. These are the substance of the Subject. The Kantian *noumenal* Self is here fused with the empirical, and is known in a fashion and a degree inside experience, though not as a pure or mere phenomenon. (*b*) Besides existence in this wide sense of actuality and factuality in the "real" world in time and space, the Subject as self-making ideality enters upon existence in a more pregnant sense. It *exists for itself* and by its own realization of itself. It is self-transcendence, it is always more than its realized expression; it is an idea, the sum of ideas, of its own possible expression, some of which it proceeds to translate into reality or actuality. Here the Subject chooses itself in freedom. *Existenz* enters here upon a new potential where the values of ethics and religion and creative art and intellect are in place. Existentialism, in the current modern sense, operates in terms of this second sense of the word existence, and presents us with varying views of man's world as dependent upon his self-realization in face of it. In the wide sense of our terminology, this is a subordination of Object to Subject, an assertion of the importance of the Subject to the Object (accompanied as we have seen by something very like its opposite, the evisceration of the substantial Subject and its interpenetration by the Object of its concerns). Is this really the exaltation of the Subject? Is subjectivity the truth in every sphere, or only in certain spheres; perhaps the highest, perhaps the final truth of things? Is the ultimate truth—the quest of philosophy and religion both—that which reality comes to mean in terms of man's self-making by means of it? What, in short, is the *revelatory* value of Existentialism, or rather, of the existentialist approach to the ontological problem? In particular, we are interested in the theological aspects of this issue. Is the existentialist emphasis an assistance towards understanding the nature of Christian truth? Is faith, which is set forth as the correlate of the truth revealed to Christian knowledge, an existentialist attitude towards the Object or Objects which it knows and from which it derives its assurance? If so, then in what manner and degree?

1

There is a sense in which the Subject modifies the Object of knowledge which is of so wide an application as to reduce the truth of the proposition to something near a truism. The Subject in the Kantian system subjects the Object to the laws of thought, to the forms of space and time and the categories of the understanding. The presuppositions of Kantianism leave open the possibility that the Object as thing-in-itself may be quite unlike its appearance to mind or consciousness. But as Object, as the thing-known, as appearance to Subject or mind, the unknowable *noumenon* has undergone modification by the nature and activity of the Subject. We may reject this dualism of thought and being in its Kantian form, and assert in some sort an original and abiding togetherness of thought and being. But Martin Heidegger is a powerful reminder that knowledge, even in its strictest form of natural science, is still a human "project." One may have some doubt whether Heidegger's quest of an ultimate ontology, to which the argument of *Sein und Zeit* is a preliminary only, is not itself an impossible attempt to think away thought from being. On his own showing can we ever get behind ontology as a "meaning," the *Sinn von Sein*? We may find reason to hold that things have being apart from thought. But to frame that being in a formula is to express their being-apart-from-thought in yet one more being-for-thought. Is not Heidegger himself caught in the relics of the Kantian dualism? His position with regard to the "objective" knowledge of natural science is a useful reminder that even such knowledge, even as knowledge, for a Subject, is modified in its objectivity by the conditions called for by the necessity of appearing to a finite mind. But such a generality casts no light upon the particular kinds and classes of objects and the degree of their implication in the Subject in the process of being known. It is like that other generality which says that everything that comes before mind is *eo ipso* an Object; a truism which leaves undistinguished fact and fancy, sanity and illusion, sober history and romantic fiction. Any sense, therefore, in which modification of the Object by the Subject is asserted, as it is asserted by the existentialist approach to philosophical problems, must, if it is to be fruitful in its illumination of the nature of our knowledge, assert this modification above the level of natural happening, something that inevitably occurs whenever any Subject knows any Object.

We call to mind in this connection that Kierkegaard tried to link his exposition of the importance of the Subject to truth with a general doctrine of the existence of the Subject as a concrete being in time and becoming. This sets the being of the Subject in flux, dissolves its substantiality into an ideality which must continually make and remake itself, resolve itself in a new substantiality of self-choice and self-creation. But this *natural* necessity of self-renewal need not be significant *ethical* self-choice, although it provides the basis for this possibility. And it is not long before it is apparent that it is such ethical choice that Kierkegaard is interested in, as the preparatory stage on life's way for the religious and the Christian, in which subjectivity, in his sense, becomes the truth. Later Existentialism makes a distinction between real and mechanical choice here. Heidegger, avoiding, as he thinks, the terminology of the ethical, talks of authentic and inauthentic existence, personal and impersonal modes of life. Buber speaks of real living and the life of relation. The Christian existentialists speak of genuine history. And so on. The subjective emphasis which, according to all these thinkers, is necessary to penetrate to the truth is a specific exercise of subjectivity, not a general and formal aspect of the relations of Subject and Object—indeed, Martin Buber asserts that real living cannot be expressed in this formula at all; for this formula is at home only in the indifferent, dispassionate, scientific nature of knowledge, where *ex hypothesi* the real life of the Subject is excluded as irrelevant. It is difficult to find any word for this specific exercise of subjectivity which makes the self relevant to truth other than just this term *ethical,* using it in the widest sense as the opposite in this context of *natural*. And what we have to consider now is how this energizing of the Subject which makes it relevant, and even all important to truth, affects the Object and the conception of objectivity.

It is difficult to resist the conclusion from the types of so-called "subjective thinking" studied in our course, that the Objects which are "made" or modified by the Subject, and where such subjective energizing is relevant to our knowledge of the Objects, are not the "objects" of the natural world, things, happenings, occurrences, apart from relation to Subjects, but those departments of existence which are Objects-in-relation-to-Subjects. "Objects," we remember, are anything that can come before mind in being known. There is a natural prejudice in favour of taking Objects as "things," material objects in the first place, the objects of daily use and meeting. We need to remind ourselves that not only can ideas and abstractions be Objects of knowledge, but that experiences, psychological and even spiritual, can be Objects of reflection and study. Even those experiences to which Martin Buber would deny the name of such, (for fear of eviscerating their significance in "psychologism"), those awarenesses of encountered *Thou-ness,* even those are *Gegenwart,* encounters of reality over against the self involved, and so imply some form of the distinction of Subject and Object. This aspect does not exhaust the experiences, and to regard them as examples of the "objective" procedure of knowledge may actually distort them. The relations of the Subject as living self to these primary Objects of awareness in encounter can themselves come before mind as Objects of a secondary sort; and at the ethical level, using the word in the wide sense indicated above, the interest and evaluation of the Subject's active relation here enter into the reality of the secondary Object, and are relevant to truth in this sphere of existence. Once more, the relations of the Subject to the Object are important for truth in those spheres where the relations of Subject to Object are themselves the matters studied.

This conclusion need not reduce the "existentialist" emphasis on the contribution of the Subject to the Object to a truism. It calls attention to the fact that religion and ethics, community life and intellectual and artistic endeavour, are not matters in which truth is *found* but is in some sort *made;* their Objects are not "there" in the same fashion as are the Objects of natural knowledge or science; they are aspects of spiritual life. As such they cannot be known apart from the Subject's active entering into them, participating in them, making them part of its substance, making itself in terms of them. It is a further question whether there is a general "objective" truth in these departments of experience, discoverable upon participation in them, disclosing or revealing its nature and laws to progressive insight. There are forms of Existentialism which deny this, which assert that the Subject must take all upon itself, make its own values, introduce its own objectivities into a material which in the end is indifferent to this injection. At any rate, the truth is not to be known in such matters apart from the Subject of dispassionate knowledge's turning itself into an active, participating energizing in what is over against it, whether as a tradition to be appropriated (as in the Christian existentialism of Kierkegaard) or an invitation or challenge in the appearance of things (as in Martin Buber's encounter of the cosmos as *Thou*) or a *kerygma* claiming divine origin and sanction (in the specifically Christian dogmatic theology of Karl Barth). The Objects or matters concerning which truth is asserted or may be known are simply not "there" apart from the Subject's entering into its own sphere of discourse.

It is not affirmed, surely, that the Subject's attitude to the Objects of natural knowledge or science modifies these in their inmost being. Both Kant and Heidegger may be regarded as asserting modification in the Object as known, in the process of submitting itself to the Subject's understanding; science is in terms of the categories and the forms of sense according to the one, is a human "project" according to the later thinker. But then knowledge is of phenomenal reality only, in Kant, and the thing-in-itself is not affected by mind's taking knowledge of it; while for Heidegger there is a background of "brute fact" which is not drawn into the schematization of the "project," and there remains the promised second instalment of his ontological quest as yet unfulfilled. There is a realm of objectivity which is not drawn into the power of the Subject to affect. If one sets out by defining objectivity as things as they are, apart from knowledge or apart from the Subject's interest in them, then two questions arise: (*a*) how far can anything at all be known or said about reality so defined? Can we think away thought from things? (*b*) what is the status of the "objective" world so defined? By what right do we call this "ultimate" reality? By what right do we deny that the values of this objective world for selves have no relevance as a clue to its nature or significance? Why should human concerns and preoccupations be subject to devaluation as "merely subjective" from the superior standard of "things-apart-from-selves"? If we cannot know things-in-themselves, we cannot know that the ultimate nature of things is either hostile or indifferent to human values. If we identify ultimate truth with the truth about objects-apart-from-selves (as it appears to us!) what is the justification of this identification of truth with indifference to human concerns? Is this more than prejudice in favour of one particular kind of knowledge? Is it not an extension of the admitted ideal of scientific procedure within its own sphere to matters outside its sphere, without any examination of the question whether there may not be other approaches to truth? It is still a question whether the Subject's involvement in the Objects of its concern may not yield insights that are relevant to the ultimate nature of things. Existentialism has got hold of the truth of the determinative significance of the Subject for the Object within certain spheres of spirituality. This is a formal principle only, and yields no more metaphysical conclusions upon ultimates than does the Subject-Object relation itself. But the content or material experienced or known within the life of spirit itself might present us with certain implications, inferences, guesses, hopes relating to its own ultimate significance, which would remain for evaluation in terms of whatever standards might appear to be available to us.

A very little reflection on modern existentialism as typified in Heidegger, and filled out with some acquaintance with Jaspers and Sartre, is enough to remind us that, for all the talk of self-making and the determinative place of the active Subject in knowledge, there is no thought, either in intention or yet in result, that the self or Subject makes the cosmos over again according to its heart's desire. Indeed, only in Buber and in the Christian existentialisms is there any suggestion that the purpose or drift of the cosmos is helped towards its realization by human self-making. For the most part the self constructs its own nest of security in the branches of an indifferent universe. Jaspers, Heidegger, Sartre, all stress the truth that this world is the only world there is, and that the scientific description of it, though limited and never complete, is true so far as it goes. For Heidegger the cardinal aspect of human existence is that it is "being for death" bounded on both sides by nothingness. In Sartre le Néant invades meaning at all points; the evisceration of human existence is complete. Self-making gives no clue to the inmost structure of the universe; rather it presupposes that the scheme of things has no meaning, or that the meaning introduced by human self-making is significant only within the context of itself. What is so made has no revelatory light to throw on the inner tendency of what offers itself for such transformation or elevation into significance. Such existentialism is as severely (if not savagely) repressive of human hope as scientific naturalism. Indeed, in Heidegger it is advanced as the objective parallel in philosophical thinking to the procedure of natural science: it is phenomenological analysis. But does such analysis necessarily have the last word in answer to human questioning regarding the ultimate reality? The results of the analysis are surely presupposed! What begins as phenomenology ends as ontology and asserts that no further metaphysical truth is open to our knowledge or faith. True, e.g. we cannot see past death, which may be allowed to have determinative significance for our thought of life, and may even be allowed to influence our thought of what constitutes "authentic existence." But, even apart from the specific grounds on which the Christian hope of immortality is based, there are features of human life which in all ages and place have suggested to man's heart that perhaps this life might not end at death. The assumption that it does so end goes beyond phenomenological analysis, and *is* an assumption—however warranted the assumption may nowadays seem in the light of scientific knowledge of the relations of body and soul. The metaphysics of Existentialism, whether in its atheistic and naturalistic or in its Christian and personalistic forms, do not appear to arise out of phenomenological analysis undertaken and performed in the spirit of objectivistic indifferentism to human hopes and fears. They have their own separate grounds. "In the history of the human spirit," writes Martin Buber, "I distinguish between epochs of habitation and epochs of homelessness. In the former, man lives in the world as in a house, as in a home. In the latter, man lives in the world as in an open field and at times does not even have four pegs with which to set up a tent."[1] And, in giving some examples of such various epochs, he makes it clear that the grounds for such feeling of being at home or without a home in the universe are themselves very various. "In the post-augustinian west it is not the contemplation of nature, as with the Greeks, but faith which builds a new house in the cosmos for the solitary soul."[2] Our present interest is in the word "faith" here. The indifference or friendliness of the universe to man is not to be decided on grounds of, or by the methods of, phenomenological analysis. There is a doubt whether the existentialist approach to ontology is capable of covering all the ground. There is even a doubt whether in Heidegger himself there is not a crack in the phenomenology where an ultimate of a different sort shines through, the appearance unwished and unexpected of an ethical element of evaluation. But dare Existentialism risk an absolute? Those forms of the current fashion seem more consistent which make the Subject responsible for the creation of its own values, indeed, for the very conception of value. This nihilism is brought up against the fact that *truth* is a value, of course. Unless all idea of objectivity is to be thrown out of doors, truth must be reinstated. And it becomes a question whether there is not a truth in the realm of the ethical; a truth which is somehow reinstated in the statement that there is no objective truth there.

It should be apparent by now that for Existentialism, in spite of all its talk of self-making, the Subject does not escape

[1] *Between Man and Man,* p. 126.
[2] *op. cit.,* p. 129.

the control of the Object, using these words in their broadest sense, and that the truth is not "what one cares to make it." On the one hand human freedom is realized within the strongest bonds of natural necessity in the set-up of each Subject's historical situation: in Sartre's formula "I am sad, French, and a waiter." The concrete Subject is thoroughly embedded in the context of his environment and destiny. The possibilities of self-realization are not infinite but very severely limited. In the end, Heidegger reminds us, death gets us all and cancels all achievement. The truth of human life, in the sense of what makes the most of this circumscribed freedom which is open to us, what tends to "authentic existence," is a truth which we make true for ourselves by self-identification with it, entering upon it in risk and commitment and so prove the trueness of by experiment ending in experience. There is, moreover, a generality of agreement in the content of such moral truth, which is only denied by the extremer forms of Existentialism which make the Subject take the responsibility for manufacturing its own standard of values, which envisage the possibility of a satanic decision in self-making "Evil, be thou my good." Except for such anarchism or nihilism, there is thus a rooting of value in existence, an objectivism set over against the subjectivity upon which stress is set. Although "I make the truth true for me" it is still true that truth is in things, and "I adjust myself to the truth." The mere fact that Heidegger wishes to present his conclusions as the outcome of phenomenological analysis untinged by ethical consideration is one more indication that truth is control by the Object, even where the truth concerned is that concerning the self-making of Subjects.

The last topic which we wish to discuss in this section concerns a certain disparagement discernible in some of the existential doctrine we have looked at of the Subject-Object relation as a form of knowledge. This is most explicit, of course, in Martin Buber; but the attitude has become more widely diffused through his influence. Thus A. A. Bowman, in *Studies in the Philosophy of Religion*,[3] writes: "The tacit assumption that experience is all of the Subject-Object type

[3] *op. cit.*, vol. ii, p. 239: quoted Dr. John Baillie, *Our Knowledge of God* (1939), p. 217.

has played havoc with much European philosophy." This is, of course, a statement about "experience," not about knowledge; and if it amounted to the position that "experience is wider than knowledge, strictly so called," then common sense as well as philosophy could readily agree. But it is implied both in common sense and in philosophy that experience involves knowledge of some kind, even if not "knowledge" in the strict sense of "scientific" or exactly verifiable knowledge. If it is meant that "experience-knowledge" is more than natural science, no one will want to cavil with such a position. If it is meant, however, that there is a knowledge which is above and superior to the Subject-Object relation, then we may well hesitate. Everything that is known is in some sense Object to a Subject—not necessarily a "real object," for it may be a hallucination; not necessarily a "material object," for it may be an abstract idea or a generalization as to the behaviour of such objects; not necessarily a "natural object," for it may be another Subject of knowledge and experience, functioning in one or other of its activities as spirit. When a modern writer can say "The scientist is concerned with the world of objects, the historian with other subjects,"[4] we must comment immediately that the "subjects" with which the historian deals are the "objects" of his knowledge. What we want to add here is that such "objects," being "subjects of knowledge and experience and action," cannot be known according to the categories appropriate to the knowledge of natural science. There is nothing inherently wrong or amiss with the form of knowledge in the Subject-Object relation. Buber tries to limit knowledge to those forms of it in which the Subject is, or may come to be, definitely distinguished from and set over against the Object. This reflective consciousness certainly implies separation of Subject and Object, in a way which falls short of the felt unity of experience or the realized "life of relation" which restores man's unity with the community or cosmos. There is a suggestion that knowledge *must* distort, and that there are other forms of "experience" (we remember Buber's objections to the psychologistic implications of this word)

[4] Adrian Coates, *A Basis of Opinion* (1938), p. 28; quoted Dr. Baillie, *loc. cit.*

which get us nearer to reality. With this latter position we can agree, on two interpretations of its meaning. Living experience is itself existence, being as compared with thought. Moreover, there is always more in life than thought can articulate in language. But is it necessarily the case that to reduce experience to knowledge is to dissipate its significance and content? Experience is surely never mindless as long as it is conscious. Something appears to awareness and is known. This will not always be a defined and delimited Object, either now or later susceptible of being set over against a clearly recognizable Subject. Still less need it always be an Object in the sense in which natural science deals with Objects. But with what right do we assert that the Subject-Object relation is appropriate to scientific knowledge only, that its introduction involves the naturalistic explanation of phenomena? Is not the antithesis of knower and thing known native to all kinds of knowledge? Can "experience" be denied this double aspect, which stamps it as a kind of knowledge; implicit perhaps, but still capable of clarification and claim to verification, i.e. as a species of truth? It is a dangerous doctrine that experience is above knowledge; for this removes it from any possible claim to throw light on the general nature of things. This is subjectivity without objectivity. All that can be said of such experience is that it happens: it is brute fact without relation or connection, throwing light on nothing, not even itself.

The characteristic terminology of Martin Buber bears witness to this state of affairs. The *Thou* still appears to an *I* in *Gegenwart*, which is literally an "over-againstness," a distinction of Subjects in relation. What is essential to his position is that when the Object is another Subject, a *Thou*, it is a different kind of Object from the Object of natural knowledge, and is known in a special way. The Subjects engage each other in their whole being; whereas in natural knowledge the Subject holds itself aloof from and indifferent to the Object, which is incapable of engaging the Subject in a living way, as a real Subject in its turn. But a real, if not a natural knowledge, emerges from the encounter—indeed, a knowledge of the most vital and important kind. Buber certainly means this knowledge to be construed as "objective" in the sense of being *true*. But the *Thou* is an Object of a special kind, and the objectivity of truth in the life of relation is a different kind of objectivity from that of natural science. It is not that of the natural occurrence of things already "there," but of phases of spiritual life which are *made* to happen, depend on the attitude of will in the Subject. This is why it seems somewhat premature to indulge in rejoicings that Buber's distinction of the words of *I-It* and *I-Thou* has destroyed the prescriptive right of the world of *I-It* to "objectivity." The world of relation is as "objective," we are told, as the compulsive reality of natural objects and the study of them in natural science. That may or may not be proved by Buber; but the objectivity is of a different order in the two spheres. The rejoicings seem after all, to take the "objectivity" of the natural order and of the truth of natural science for the type of such obvious, compulsive, undeniable truth, and to find that the truth of the life of relation, which Buber himself described as the life of spirit, partakes of the kind of objectivity which attaches to material things and happenings. The objectivity of the life of the spirit or relation still needs to be shown in its ultimate reference by other kinds of argument than the particular variety of phenomenological analysis in which Buber operates in his distinction of *I-It* and *I-Thou* attitudes and worlds.

In concluding this section it may also be remarked that the two distinctively Christian thinkers we have studied, Kierkegaard, usually hailed (with what reservations as to the justness of the description we have earlier noted) as the "father of Existentialism," and Karl Barth, whose disclaimer of Existentialism as a philosophy does not prevent the presence of existentialist elements in his construction, that neither of these can be quoted as polemizing against the Subject-Object relation as such. Kierkegaard did conceive that certain modifications in the traditional logic might be called for when the Subject of knowledge was existentially set in the flux of becoming in time—modifications in the spirit of the Aristotelian logic rather than the Platonic conception of the eternity of truth which found its contemporary representation in the Hegelian philosophy. But this modification did not appear to him as calling for the abandonment of the Subject-Object form of knowledge. The living, acting, suffering Subject, whose energizing is necessary to the highest realization of truth as subjectivity, is yet occupied with an Object over against it, which offers matter for precise definition in its uniqueness. Both sides of the relation in which living Christianity consists he continues to the end to describe in the terminology of the Subject-Object relation. As for the Barthian dogmatics, the terminology of Subject and Object is there fundamental. Indeed, the relation which we have seen is properly at home within as epistemology is elevated by him into an ontology, and becomes the key to the inner nature of the Godhead in Trinity of Persons. Not man only is a Subject knowing Objects, but God Himself is supreme Subject offering Himself to Himself as Object in God the Son in the unity of God the Holy Spirit. God likewise offers Himself to man's faith-knowledge as Object in the revelation of the event called Jesus Christ, a particular course of historical happening which operates for faith as signifying the saving work of God for man, so guaranteeing the objectivity of the truth revealed as the very truth of God Himself, His presence and working. If something different from the epistemological sense of Subject is meant in the teaching that in so becoming Object to man's faith-knowledge God is still "indefeasibly Subject," if this is an echo of grammatical usage rather than Kantian epistemology, still the treatment of salvation as a kind of *knowledge* (*Glaubenserkenntnis*) keeps even this terminology of Subject-Object close to its philosophical origins.

2

We now turn to a consideration of what light is thrown upon the nature and functioning of faith in the Christian scheme of salvation by such existentialist discussion as we have examined. In the context of our exposition the question may be formulated thus: how far does Christian theology conceive that in *faith* the Subject makes its Object?

It is the special characteristic of the Christian forms of existentialist thought which we have examined—in Kierkegaard, in Karl Barth, in our slight reference to Rudolf

Bultmann—that the *Existenz* of the Subject is determined by a particular, even a unique Object. The distinctive matter in specific Christianity is the proclamation of a gospel, of certain saving acts of God which are set before men as a message to which they are called upon to respond. There is an original *kerygma,* there is a tradition deriving therefrom, which presents men with an Object to which their subjectivity adjusts itself, but which comes before them in the first instance as something which they did not themselves make or discover. The Object is not a generalization regarding total experience towards which the Subject has found itself disposed by certain of its moods or attitudes, not a possible way of regarding the universe, nor a permissible pattern of human life and action to which the concrete nature of the human Subject has made its contribution, conscious or unconscious. Indeed, in Kierkegaard the opposite of such a point of view is pressed to the absolute limit: the Object is inconceivable paradox; it is what never entered into the heart of man, what runs counter to all the immanent course of his thought, and what remains scandal or offence to his natural reason. In Karl Barth the opposition of transcendence to immanence remains characteristic of the Object; for though mediated by particular sensuous natural objects and occurrences, the Object is God Himself who remains ineluctably Subject. Apart from the particular self-revelation of this one living and true God in Jesus Christ there is no Object for faith to discover or invent or make its contribution to, anywhere. The absolute otherness of the Object to the human Subject seems to be asserted in terms which correspond to Barth's endeavour to rid his *Dogmatik* from the influence and terminology of the existentialist philosophy.

How comes it then that Kierkegaard can be hailed as "the father of Existentialism"; that Karl Barth is careful and anxious to remove the traces of Existentialism from the exposition of his dogmatics; that Rudolf Bultmann can present a version of the gospel on the basis of a Heideggerian prolegomena; that Paul Tillich can greet "the rise of Existentialism" as "a providential occasion for theology,"[5] and

[5] *Syllabus of Gifford Lectures, 1953,* p. 5.

entitle his first course of Gifford Lectures at Aberdeen "Existential Questions and Theological Answers"?

It is part of the answer to all such questions, of course, that, whatever the determinative place of the Object in Christian faith, yet faith is an exercise of human subjectivity. As a form of spirituality, as belonging to the phenomenology of religion, as an attitude, a disposition, an activity of the human will, as the "faith working by love" and issuing in hope, as the appropriation of tradition and *kerygma* with its resultant expression in life and action, doing and suffering within the Christian pathos, quite obviously and undeniably faith is an energizing of the human Subject which "makes the truth true for me," for the Subject concerned. Religion is life. It is one grand aspect of Kierkegaard's prophetic witness to his own contemporary Denmark and to Christianity everywhere, that the Christian life is not natural occurrence nor natural inheritance, not quasi-physical incorporation in an historical institution. Faith is not wrought *ex opere operato*: it is the supreme exercise of subjectivity. It cannot *be* true, as elements in a naturally existing tradition: it is *made* true, realized as true, as it is appropriated as truth in a form of living. This is most certainly the case on the subjective side of the relation. As the truth of a certain kind of life the Christian life must be lived in order to constitute its own truth. It is a form of the Subject's self-making. But it is also true of the verification of the objective content of faith: obedience is the organ of spiritual knowledge. Whether the Object of faith be conceived as a self-contained sphere of experience or as a realm of divine transcendence, a form of communion with realities beyond the phenomenal sensuous elements of our environment; in either case verification must await upon entering upon the conditions which the Object itself prescribes. Choice, commitment, experiment precede experience.

The fundamental importance of the Subject's part in giving reality to religious truth in the energizing of faith must not be conceived as in any way invalidated or even diminished by Kierkegaard's teaching that "the paradox gives the condition" for its own appropriation, or by Karl Barth's insistence that revelation extends the *Existenz* of the human Subject of faith-knowledge by a dimension which makes possible its own reception in faith and obedience to the divine Subject revealed. Both are ways of asserting that the Christian knowledge and enjoyment of God are brought about by God's own initiative and free grace: the total disposition and economy within which this converse of man and God takes place, in its beginning, continuance, and ending, are God's doing, not man's. In Kierkegaard the contrast with all that the human Subject can know and do by and of himself is secured by making God's entry into history for man's salvation the unique paradox which runs counter to all that man has experience of elsewhere. In Karl Barth God is indefeasibly Subject in all His making of Himself Object to man's perception, for man's self-surrender to in the obedience of faith. But neither statement of the absolute priority of God in man's knowledge and enjoyment of Him is meant as denial of the psychological subjecthood of the man of faith. Religion, even the Christian religion with its doctrine of God the Holy Spirit in the hearts of believers, the power and principle of a new life, this too is genuine human experience; venture and adventure in faith, according to Barth; a supreme passion of subjectivity hanging on to God in face of complete objective uncertainty, according to Kierkegaard; in both calling for all the powers of man's will, patience, endurance. Neither intends the elimination of human effort, rather its enlargement by a whole diameter of being. What both assert is the incompetence of man to discover or provide himself with this truth and life, apart from the particular prior and continuing act of God in Jesus Christ. Kierkegaard wishes the reduction of philosophic pride in German idealism. Karl Barth intends the refutation of natural theology and humanistic religiosity. The very ability of the human Subject to assent to the incredible propositions of the gospel is a function of his being to which the gospel raises him in proposing itself for his acceptance. He truly accepts; but his acceptance is "bracketed within" the enabling, soliciting, disposing proposal of God. Thus human subjecthood has new light thrown upon it, new scope and power added to it, by the action of the divine Subject.

More, however, is meant in Kierkegaard and Karl Barth

both, by the existentialist features in their constructions (for these are present, whether or not they represent or repudiate Existentialism) than that the Subject of faith must act or react upon the Object of saving knowledge in order that Christian life may come into existence as a department of psychological reality or spiritual experience. In some sort an activity of the Subject is requisite to the recognition of the truth of the Object; and it remains further to ask whether this activity of the Subject in any sense *makes* the truth of the Object. Is truth in the context of Christian faith and life in any sense a piece of existentialist "self-making"?

The intention of both Christian thinkers referred to is surely to present us with opposite of this last suggestion. For all his talk of subjectivity as truth, Kierkegaard presents us with a version of the Christian life determined by an Object which man does not in any sense make or construct or even accidentally or incidentally discover. However strenuous an activity faith may be, it is a passion called into being by an Object of supreme concern; an Object which presents itself in a fashion apart from and counter to all experience else; an incredible Object which is declared true and the highest, most ultimate truth. The faith which responds to the paradox of the Eternal entering history in a particular Man is in a sense the self-emptying of the Subject, not its self-making: it is allowing oneself to be made by the Object. Faith of this kind is "a condition given by the paradox." So, too, in Karl Barth, objectivity in Christian faith and obedience is given by the real subjectivity or subjecthood of God in revelation in Jesus Christ: human subjecthood is secondary, is response in a dimension of human *Existenz* created, "called forth" (*hervorgerufen*), by the divine Object which is throughout active Subject.

But when we come to examine more closely the representations of both writers on the genesis of faith, the matter is not quite so simple. Thus, in Kierkegaard, the Object which manifests itself in so completely objective a fashion as to inspire the highest activity and passion of subjectivity in the man of faith is: (*a*) paradox, (*b*) the entrance of the paradox into history; the problem is how can an historical occurrence propose itself as Object of saving faith? For, observe, the separation of these two aspects of the Object does not imply duality in the Object. The Object is not paradoxical in and of itself, but only in its entrance into history. That the Eternal should enter into time, clothe itself in an individual Man living at a particular epoch in historical time and in geographical space, is paradoxical to our idea of time and the usual, immanental, Platonic conception of eternity. It is not surprising, therefore, that Kierkegaard has such difficulty in setting forth this unique "historical consciousness" which proposes itself as the basis of saving knowledge. He has already defined history as "approximation knowledge": its best conclusion is a probability, progressively weakened by distance in time from the historical event. *The entrance into time of Eternity cannot be shown historically,* as an historical event; for this conception of Eternity is the negation of history. The paradox cannot appear as such historically: it is the end, the supersession of history. Hence all the shifts in Kierkegaard's picture of the "historical Jesus." A faithful record of all the doings, a complete transcript of all the sayings of Jesus, would not disclose the divinity of Jesus, he says. No! for the divinity of Jesus, the entrance in Him of God into the world, of the Eternal into time, is not an historical event at all. It is something which is not event: it is a divine dimension of events which is not apparent historically. It is a significance, a meaning, a value attributed to events, to a life, to the words and deeds and birth and death of Jesus; a significance, meaning, value, which can and do escape some or even many. Is the faith to which they are apparent or revealed or vouchsafed or disclosed, is this to be classed as divine gift not further to be understood but merely accepted as such; or is it to be appreciated by assimilation to other processes of conviction on ultimate matters, with which we are acquainted? In particular, is the attaching of significance to the historical matter here in question a contribution from the side of the Subject to the Object?

A similar ambiguity attaches to Karl Barth's representations on the objectivity of God in revelation. God reveals Himself in the event of Jesus Christ (which includes its preparation in the history of Israel, whose Messiah He is and in its continuation in the Church of the Apostles down through the Christian centuries) by means of actual concrete objects perceptible to our human senses, elements in our geographical and historical environment. These act as *signs*, so that their objectivity signifies the divine objectivity. But they do not do this to all and sundry. To the unbelieving the signs fail of their signification, and so remain pieces of purely secular happening. Even to the believing their function of signifying does not destroy their creaturely objectivity. They veil as well as reveal the divine Object, who is here also Subject. Thus salvation-history is not so much *Geschichte* as *Urgeschichte*. Plain history, in Barth as in Kierkegaard, does not yield the dimension of *significance*, which is that in which faith lives and operates. This concept of *Urgeschichte* is difficult and ambiguous: to an unsympathetic critic it is "a sort of eternal essence of occurrences that never occurred."[6] At any rate it shows that the feature in Christian history which is all-important for faith cannot be demonstrated or verified except to and for faith itself. The word *sign* as used by Barth suggests a further difficulty. Ordinarily, signs function within a convention, where a familiar and intelligible object suggests a less familiar or more difficult object, partly or dimly known; but still *known*. Barth wishes the objects which in revelation are divinely chosen to be signs of the divine objectivity to suggest an Object not otherwise known. But signification cannot be from a known object out into a blank void. The connection between sign and thing signified cannot be totally arbitrary. This, of course, is a problem arising rather within the context of Barth's polemic against natural theology. It suggests that the signs in revelation must link up with something already if vaguely known, guessed, surmised about a possible or probable God; which something here come to assist the elucidation of signification in the creaturely symbols. It still remains true that natural or historical happening, as such, is not enough for supernatural signification.

Inevitably we are reminded here of an earlier controversy. The Ritschlian construction of the Christian Faith insisted on a distinction between judgements of fact and judgements

[6] John Laird, *Theism and Cosmology*, 1939, p. 37.

of value as necessary to express the special quality of the asseverations of that faith and experience. For faith Jesus Christ "has the value of God." The vogue of philosophies of value has somewhat receded in recent times. But it is possible to trace the vestigial survival of the term "value" in new derivatives from the Heideggerian *Sorge*. "Concern" is a key word, for example, in the theological vocabulary of Paul Tillich. "Theology deals with what concerns us inescapably, ultimately, unconditionally . . . Without the element of ultimate concern no assertion is a theological one."[7] The Ritschlian school, by defining theology as a "practical discipline," wrongly sets this in opposition to theory, and wishing to cut theology off from philosophy thereby sacrifices truth to morals. But "truth is an essential element in what concerns us ultimately."[8] Our concern with Jesus Christ is therefore an aspect of our finding ultimate meaning in Him. It is a further question—and a fundamental one, perhaps the very issue of the relevance of the existentialist approach itself —whether the concern finds the significance or the significance creates the concern! At all events Tillich does not conceive that history as such can yield the value or concern which faith attributes to Jesus Christ. In an early work he tells us that he "attempted to answer the question, how the Christian doctrine might be understood, if the non-existence of the historical Jesus should become historically probable. Even today, I maintain the radicalism of this question over against compromises . . . The foundation of Christian belief is not the historical Jesus, but the biblical picture of Christ. The criterion of human thought and action is not the constantly changing and artificial product of historical research, but the picture of Christ as it is rooted in ecclesiastical belief and human experience."[9] This passage may be taken to illustrate an ambiguity in the formula "the historical Jesus." The detail of the construction of the historical facts of the mission and message of Jesus (including the extreme finding that the tradition of these is completely unhistorical and that Jesus never lived or taught at all) does change

[7] *The Protestant Era*, 1951, p. 98.
[8] *loc. cit.*
[9] *The Interpretation of History*, 1936, p. 33f.

from one scholar of New Testament origins to another. Faith cannot wait on the completion and certification of historical research, which is "approximation knowledge" in Kierkegaard's term. But "the historical Jesus" may also mean "the fact of Jesus' actual appearance in history," the "historicity of Jesus," apart from any or all the detail of His actual life and work. And it is a question whether faith is indifferent to the historical Jesus in the sense that He actually was born, lived and died, suffered under Pontius Pilate, rose again on the third day following His passion. It is possible that a minimum of such historicity is sufficient to support a genuine and vigorous faith. Kierkegaard appears to stand for such a faith of the minimum; witness his remark regarding the *nota bene* of the page of universal history.[10] He bases such faith on the testimony of contemporary faith, and so introduces one more element of history; the transmission of the tradition of this contemporary witness is a link in the chain of approximation knowledge. But this additional evidence that faith is never, first or last, the product of mere historical acquaintance, cannot disguise the fact that the historicity of Jesus' actual life and death are part of the content of Christian faith as he conceives it: the incarnation, the appearance of the eternal in time as an individual Man, namely, the particular historical human being called Jesus of Nazareth, really happened, is "true history," is historically true.

This conception of the centrality of the historicity of Jesus for faith may or may not be correct or justifiable, but it is not impugned by any statement, however true, that the object of Christian faith is "the biblical picture of Christ," not the current results of criticism of the Gospels. These must not be set against one another as mutually incompatible or even indifferent. The classical conception in Christian theology of the relations of faith to history requires that the Christ of faith should be positively related to the Jesus of history. History must be capable of containing and must actually have contained the real presence of Godhead. Hence, though history as such cannot yield this conviction, it must contain the possibility of, leave room for, such conviction. The birth of the vital spark which generates faith in contact with

[10] *supra*, p. 62.

history, however the mystery be conceived, lies in another order of explanation than the historical. But, being born, it will influence the historical judgement of the believer. It will not, or should not, lead him to manipulate or manufacture history to support his faith; but it may quite well lead him to pragmatic decisions in matters which are historically doubtful. It is considerations of this sort which have led some theologians to state that the evidence for the resurrection of Jesus is moral rather than historical. "Moral" is perhaps the wrong word, suggesting that conviction is arrived at on the basis of experience other than religious, apart from the Christian revelation itself. To others' minds this may suggest "wishful thinking." There is no means of disproving the imputation other than to point to the tradition itself as a whole; to the elements of historical probability, to the fact that the tradition apparently arose out of matters that actually happened, however they be understood; to the improbability of the tradition's having arisen apart from the fact that the events it narrates really did occur; and so on. Here are in place the old arguments from the credibility of the witnesses and the transformation effected in their lives. Here is also in place the effect which the plain story of Jesus in the Gospels still makes on unsophisticated minds not predisposed to disbelieve it. Such a pragmatic resolution of historical doubt is in order in many departments of life and thought where it is not accused of self-deception. So long as it is emphasized that its own certitude is not of the order of historical compulsion, faith can surely be allowed its own method of arriving at assurance in matters historical. Can it be shown that the processes of scientific historians are altogether free from such "subjective" bias?

The "truth" then, which "is an essential element in what concerns us ultimately," according to Paul Tillich, is not the truth of certain historical happenings. Yet his setting truth here in opposition to matters of practice and morals, which is condemned as the error of the Ritschlian school, indicates that the existentialist elements in his own approach to theological problems do not mean that truth is a value *we* confer. There is somehow a value we *find* which it concerns us ultimately to know. The balance in faith of elements which we make and find respectively is very different in Tillich from Barth's account of the matter, and it may help to clear our minds on this all-important topic, which is also the main theme of this concluding section of our study, to follow Tillich's representations further.

"Theology asks for the ultimate ground and power and norm and aim of being, as far as it is *my* being and carries *me* as the abyss and ground of my existence . . . in asking for the meaning of being, theology asks for God . . . it asks for the way in which man receives or resists the appearance of his ultimate concern."[11] "Theology thinks on the basis of the existential situation and in continuous relation to it."[12] We noted earlier[13] that *Existenz* in modern philosophical and theological usage usually stands for a power or potency of human being, not for its merely factual existence (although in considering Kierkegaard we found that this latter aspect is important in his polemic against Hegel). Tillich identifies the quest of theology with the quest of *significance* in human beings, with a Heideggerian attempt on "the meaning of being," and the "being" in question is "human being" as in the case of Heidegger's *Dasein*. This meaning is "God." But it is important to note what this signifies! " 'God' is the answer to the question implied in man's finitude; he is the name for that which concerns man ultimately. This does not mean that first there is a being called God and then the demand that man should be ultimately concerned about him. It means that whatever concerns a man ultimately becomes god for him."[14] This is "a phenomenological description of the nature of the gods . . . the gods are not objects within the context of the universe. They are expressions of the ultimate concern which transcends the cleavage between subjectivity and objectivity. It remains to be emphasized that an ultimate concern is not 'subjective.' Ultimacy stands against everything which can be derived from mere subjectivity, nor can the unconditional be found within the entire catalogue

---

[11] *The Protestant Era*, p. 98f.
[12] *ibid*.
[13] *supra*, p. 43.
[14] *Systematic Theology*, Vol. 1, 1953, p. 2.

of finite objects which are conditioned by each other."[15]
This position is conscious of itself in its departures from the
classical tradition in Christian theology. God and the divine
are descriptions of reality in so far as and where man finds
his true being, his ultimate significance and meaning.
Theology is phenomenological description of the human
existential situation in regard to the ultimate meaning of
man's being. Tillich would be aware of the possible criticism
of his position from the standpoint of more traditional
theology (say, of Barthianism) that this is to make theology
a department of anthropology. But the older approach, he
might say, is no longer possible. God cannot be demonstrated
as an objective reality apart from man's concern. This is in
any case to reduce him to an item in his universe, one thing
amongst others. It does not express the involvement of the
reality which man calls God with man's own being, all those
features which in Buber, for instance, lead to the naming of
the face of the universe as Thou, thus challenging that response which alone penetrates to significance and meaning.
If it be objected that this is a theology of immanence, Tillich
could reply that he offers his own version of transcendence
(as belonging to the very nature of the human subject of
religion); and he does retort upon the Barthian position as
"supra-naturalism."[16] "Self-transcending realism" is his name
for his own position, and of this he writes that it "requires
the criticism of all forms of supra-naturalism . . . in the
sense of a theology that imagines a supra-natural world be-
side or above the natural one, a world in which the unconditional finds a local habitation, thus making God a transcendent object, the creation an act at the beginning of time,
the consummation a future state of things. To criticize such a
conditioning of the unconditional, even if it leads to atheistic
consequences, is more religious, because it is more aware of
the unconditional character of the divine, than a theism
which bans God into the supra-natural realm."[17]

It is possible that the situation is not quite so simple as all
this. It is certainly a great convenience to have a God who

[15] loc. cit.
[16] The Interpretation of History, p. 34.
[17] The Protestant Era, p. 92.

does not have to be proved but only described as an aspect of human existence. But the ultimacy of such an ultimate remains in some doubt. The factual existence of divine power and significance is set over against demonic distortion and destruction of meaning in Tillich's own scheme. Apart from all question whether "a finite universe" is so contradictory a notion as it seems, whether "nature" is not a limited phenomenon set in a "supernature" which transcends it every way, it is not the case that the "supra-naturalist" "bans God into" this second realm above this world. And it is still more important to raise, even if we do not finally answer, the question whether God's existence for himself, his providence, his answering of prayer, his concern for us and not just our concern for and with him, whether these things are not better conserved, in the sense in which they have mattered to Christian faith, by a concept of God which we must frankly call "supra-natural."

" 'God' is the answer to the question implied in man's finitude; he is the name for that which concerns man ultimately."[18] Were it not for our knowledge of the Heideggerian background to the term "concern," for our awareness of the existentialist approach to ontological problems in terms of "self-making," the reading of being as "meaning for human existence," such a statement as this of Tillich's here would have a much more "objective" ring about it. But immediately we are warned that "This does not mean that first there is a being called God and then the demand that man should be ultimately concerned about him. It means that whatever concerns a man ultimately becomes god for him, and conversely, it means that a man can be concerned ultimately only about what is god for him."[19] This sounds like a return to subjectivity. Does Tillich really mean so? Just as we have resigned ourselves to taking his position to be "that which factually man concerns himself with as his ultimate is god for him, and 'god' has no meaning outside such factual concern," then Tillich confronts us with the statement "truth is an essential element in what concerns us ultimately."[20] Here

[18] P. Tillich, *Systematic Theology,* p. 234.
[19] *loc. cit.*
[20] *The Protestant Era,* p. 98.

is a determination of concern from the side of the Object and not the Subject of religion. Yet it is not an Object which "first exists" independently of human concern. "It is the correlate of an unconditional concern but not a 'highest thing' called 'the absolute' or 'the unconditioned,' about which we could argue in detached objectivity. It is the object of total surrender, demanding also the surrender of our subjectivity while we look at it. It is a matter of infinite passion and interest (Kierkegaard), making us its object whenever we try to make it our object. For this reason we have avoided terms like '*the* ultimate,' '*the* unconditioned,' '*the* universal,' '*the* infinite,' and have spoken of ultimate, unconditional, total, infinite concern. Of course, in every concern there is *something* about which one is concerned . . ."[21] Not only, we must insist, "something about which one is concerned," factually, but "something which reveals, declares, manifests itself as a valid object of concern." If "the truth is an essential element in which concerns us ultimately," this must surely mean that the ultimacy, too, is seen in the Object. Even allowing for the implication of the Object in man's concern, so that we do not even enter upon the sphere of religion apart from this human reference, there must be some quality in that which is taken up by man into his ultimate concern which fits the object for this evaluation; and, we must add, fits some such objects more than others, perhaps fits only one such Object for the ultimate place, using the word "ultimate" in all its seriousness. Which is as much as to say, "there must be some transition from the factual 'gods' of man's concern to the 'God' who is his highest good and only lasting satisfaction." So much seems to come of admitting "truth" as an element in what concerns us ultimately.

This does not of itself resolve the question of the independent existence of the supreme religious Object, does not clear the question between theism and pantheism, does not settle the problem of a "personal" God. "In classical theology, 'person' was used only for the three principles in the divine life, not for God himself . . . the idea of God . . . united personal with supra-personal traits . . . in the degree to which . . . God became one person alongside others . . . he was

[21] *Systematic Theology*, p. 15.

superfluous."[22] It does put a distinction between that which man concerns himself with unconditionally, whether mistakenly or otherwise, and that which man must, should or ought to concern himself with (whether the imperative in the "ought" here be conceived as categorical or hypothetical). There is a quality in things, in the Object, in the world as experienced religiously, which lays claim to and hold upon his attention as significant, as satisfying, as the bearer of his own meaning, the infinity of his own being from which he is by fate or fault actually separated. Whether this Object so revealed is active on its own account so to engage his attention or claim his loyalty; whether the Object of religion is concerned for its part in him as he in it, is a further question. And one, we must add in candour, which at this level of discussion, in the generalities of his definition of religion as "ultimate concern," Tillich does not seem to answer in the affirmative. Much of what is said reminds us of the final ambiguity on this point which we saw in Martin Buber. Whether this is an ambiguity inherent in the existentialist approach to theological problems, and one which might conceivably be corrected or amended by other considerations, remains a further question.

However these things may be, Tillich desires to come before us as a *kerygmatic,* even a Christian theologian: he is the interpreter of a message, a message of salvation, the Christian message or gospel. How is the transition effected from the generalities of religious definition to this concrete and particular objectification? In the first place, Tillich has his own version of particularization in the Object of religious faith. "It is impossible to be concerned about something which cannot be encountered concretely, be it in the realm of reality or in the realm of imagination. Universals can become matters of ultimate concern only through their power of representing concrete experiences. The more concrete a thing is, the more the possible concern about it. The completely concrete being, the individual person, is the object of the most radical concern—the concern of love."[23] Since Tillich's

[22] *The Protestant Era*, p. 70.
[23] *Systematic Theology*, p. 235.

position is a realism[24] "Religion tries to surpass the given
reality in order to approach the unconditional."[25] This means
that in reality, not in imaginary realms, but in some or
other of its concrete manifestations, not in universals or abstractions from experience, there are to be met with elements
which bear significance as revealing man's essential being,
which therefore mediate *saving* power. The "ultimate ground
and power and norm and aim of being, as far as it is my
being and carries me as the abyss and ground of my existence," which is what "theology asks for," and "in asking for
the meaning of being, theology asks for God,"[26] this particularizes itself in concrete happenings, so that "man receives or
resists the appearance of his ultimate concern."[27] It is not said
that a theistically conceived God reveals Himself in a particular line of historical happening directed towards a climax of
revelation. Rather the statements remind us of Martin Buber's
revelation of the eternal *Thou* in the particular *Thous* of
man's encounter, not involving "a self-definition of God
before men."[28] But the finding of "the object of most radical
concern" in "the completely concrete being, the individual
person" prepares us for the statement that the revelation of
the "ultimate ground and power and norm and aim of being"
as far as it is the ground and abyss of human being and *my*
being is made in one particular, individual, unique, historical
human being, Jesus of Nazareth. And since these features
are the marks of what theology calls *God,* according to
Tillich, it follows that the believing statement "Jesus is the
Christ" means that Jesus is the revelation of God: He is "the
manifestation of the essential unity between God and man
(essential God-manhood)."[29] Thus the general possibility of
particularization present in reality of the disclosure of itself
as the carrying ground and abyss of man's meaning is concentrated and realized in a unique instance and happening.

[24] See *The Protestant Era,* Chapter V, where it is defined as
"self-transcending realism," combining two elements, "the emphasis on the real and the transcending power of faith," p. 75.
[25] *op. cit.,* p. 89.
[26] *op. cit.,* p. 98f.
[27] *loc. cit.*
[28] *I and Thou,* p. 111.
[29] *Syllabus* to First Series of Gifford Lectures, Lecture VI.

This is Tillich's version of the Kierkegaardian paradox, the entrance of infinity into the finite, paradoxical not because absurd, but as "a reality which contradicts any expectation."[30]

Tillich makes this statement of the significance of Jesus within the theological circle of commitment to faith; not the willed determination of a doctrinal principle as true, or even "true for me," temporarily, provisionally, experimentally, awaiting upon verification, but in the sense of entering upon the range of realities revealed as significant, and thus the appropriation of their savingness, or satisfaction. The Object reveals its reality, significance, saving power for the Subject. Now in actual life man is estranged from his own infinity, his factual existence fighting against his essential being, meaning, true life. What in Jesus brings faith to find in Him the Christ is the disclosure to faith of a unique dimension of reality, namely, a revelation of New Being; human being, of course, or rather the factual reality of the restored unity of finite human life with its infinite ground or perfection, in which "the conflict of essential and existential being is overcome," "the appearance of a new reality within and against existence."[31] "Christian faith is created by the reality which shines through this picture," the picture of Jesus as the Christ, in the New Testament, the tradition of the Church, the consciousness of the individual believer.[32] "The Christ is the final and all embracing answer to the question implied in existence."[33] The appearance in existence of such an answer to the question posed and implied in all human existence, this revelation of New Being within and against reality, guarantees in the only sense in which we can desire or conceive guarantee and confirmation, the *truth* of the Christian claim. It is a truth manifestly appearing as such in a unique Object, yet a truth for and of a Subject's existence: it is a truth going beyond or underneath the distinction of subjective and objective, according to Tillich; for "ultimate

[30] *loc. cit.*
[31] *Syllabus,* Lectures VI and VIII.
[32] *ibid.,* Lecture VIII.
[33] *ibid.,* Lecture VI.

concern" "transcends the cleavage between subjectivity and objectivity."[34]

It thus appears that Tillich shares with Barth a tradition, the Christian tradition, written, institutional, experiential. His theology, too, is a function of the Church. But it is not an orthodox theology. Orthodoxy is a hardening of a particular answer or interpretation of the Christian answer to man's existential situation in terms of a situation which is no longer our situation. There must be correlation of theological answers to particular existential situations, to men's conception of the nature of human being and its problems in the varying historic cultural contexts. Tillich also refuses the term "dogmatics" in favour of "systematic theology." He thus resists various intellectual petrifactions of the Object of Christian faith in view of the inalienable essential reference of the Object here to the Subject's existence. Theology must never forget that its Objects exist always and only in their reference *for us*.

For many of us this reference, while it sheds a flood of light on the nature and genesis of theological statement, must continue to seem a limitation. It is a great benefit to have faith more closely involved in the very being of its Object, as one side of an existential situation for which neither Subject nor Object exist in their separation (i.e. so far as the existential situation is concerned!). But while this account seems to deal fairly enough with the phenomenology of religion, does it do justice to the ontological and (if the traditional endeavour of philosophical thought be still allowed possible) to the metaphysical implications of religion? We are warned against erecting the objects of religion into a supra-natural sphere of reality, duplicating in some sort the "things which do appear." Transcendence now has an immanent significance: it is the background of infinity against which finitude knows itself as such. "Metaphysical" is in many quarters a term of abuse. But we are reminded that in the fountainhead of modern Existentialism, in Martin Heidegger, phenomenological analysis confesses itself only the first stage of ontology. And in religion, in the Christian faith, is it possible to rest content with the bare fact (another example

[34] *Systematic Theology*, p. 238.

of "brute fact"!) that in Jesus who is called the Christ, man's existential estrangement is overcome, his being is exhibited reconciled with its essential infinity, meaning and existence are brought together in one? Why should this happen at all; why only once; why here in this particular person? Is there no intentionality in this happening? Are all such "whys" and "hows" to be disallowed as "questions not to be asked"? Are they to be dismissed as survivals of anthropomorphic mythical thinking? Is the universe to be accepted as a going concern, and the principle discarded that "things which are seen were not made of things which do appear"?[35]

It is a serious matter to have to set aside the existence of God, for and of Himself, and not just as one pole of the religious relation of human existence. What is the significance of the fact that the nature of the universe lends itself to the appearing of this relation, brings forth human beings for whom this feature is the meaning of their characteristic "existence"? Has the existential approach to theology, which sets forth this feature of the mutual involvement of Subject and Object in the religious relation, with much resulting enlightenment on the phenomenology of religion, in particular in regard to the nature, place and operation of faith therein, has not this approach gone beyond its limits in pronouncing a ban on the metaphysical impulse hitherto regarded as inherent in this experience of the ultimate? Are we not left with a major problem in the relation of such an interpretation of religious experience to the scientific account of the phenomenal world? Not, indeed, that this is an easy task on any alternative view! But does not the working out of a consistent existentialist approach to theology, and the disclosure of a fundamental opposition in the views of Tillich to the rival modern interpretation of the classical tradition (not to say the orthodox) of Christian doctrine in Barth, does not this situation invite us to consider further the presuppositions of this approach? This is a matter, of course, for the general philosopher, as well as for the theologian. The question seems to be: is it an illusion that, as has generally been held hitherto, by the exercise of his reason man can step outside the limits of his own finitude to a more

[35] Heb. 11.2.

than humanly conditioned knowledge of the nature of the reality in which he finds himself? Or has Existentialism demonstrated beyond a doubt the humanistic circle, the reference to human existence (*Dasein*) in all human knowledge? Must all statement take place within the bracketing condition "so it appears to man"? Or does the trans-subjective reference in all knowledge of an Object by a Subject ever really introduce us to things as they are in themselves, by themselves, and in some cases, for themselves? Martin Buber has familiarized us with the encounter with the *Thou,* in which the world begins all over again and exists all over again for another as it does for myself. Yet there is but *one* world. To assert the self-existence of God, the real being of things, persons, values for Him, His real activity and intentionality in relationship with His creatures, does not seem therefore necessarily to make Him one amongst others, to degrade Him in one item in His universe. This is but one issue, although an all-important one. The self-existence of God could be conceived as providing the dimension of a supernature, a metaphysical sphere in which various ultimate questions may be presumed to find their answer, which even the existentialist approach cannot non-suit, though it may ignore. If the Object may not swallow up the Subject without the destruction of spirituality, neither may the Subject presume to exhaust the Object without danger to the rooting of meaning in reality. The debate on the value of the existentialist approach to truth predominantly in terms of the Subject must continue yet awhile.

Index of Names

Note: under Barth, Buber, Heidegger, Kierkegaard, no references are given to those chapters in which each is specially and individually treated, nor to the concluding chapter where all are conjointly discussed.